Paraphrase lost?

–

Paraphrase regained

Snowdrops at Settrington Church North Yorkshire

Paraphrase lost?

–

Paraphrase regained

Poetry based on Biblical texts with
accompanying Reflections and
Christian study

David Blessing

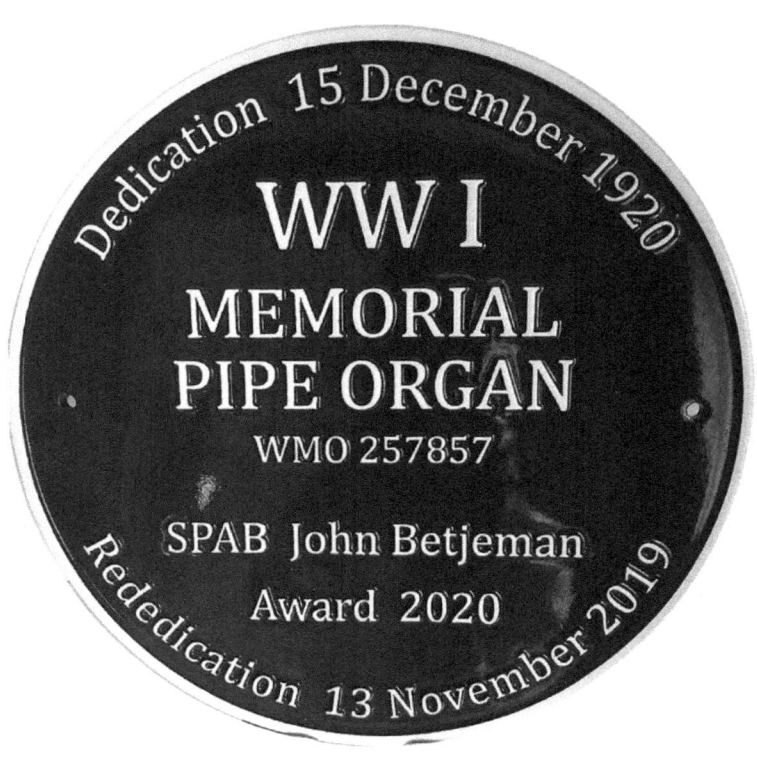

The Heritage Plaque mentioned on the back cover

First published in Great Britain in 2011
This edition published in 2021
by The Cloister House Press

ISBN 978-1-913460-47-1

Rievaulx Abbey North Yorkshire

PREFACE

This little book of poems and meditations has grown unintentionally over a number of decades. The author (writing under the pseudonym *Blessing* to avoid confusion with the common name *Smith*) first wrote a poem for his church magazine around 1970 when, having been caught unexpectedly in a sudden storm, he was moved by what he had observed. Others followed from time to time but some still lay hidden away as the years passed by.

The anthology draws on Biblical texts from Genesis and the creation story to The Revelation of John and mankind's ultimate reunion with his Creator in the New Jerusalem. As it is written in varying styles from the simplistic to the more deeply theological, it is hoped that child, teacher or preacher may find something to appeal or wish to study the Bible with a new openness of heart or freshness of mind. Written mainly in light-hearted vein, yet still serious in nature, the meditations are intended to supplement and complement each poem. The author has tried to keep closely to biblical text and true paraphrase. He has avoided, wherever possible, outmoded words and phrases, the allegoric verse form popular in hymns of previous generations, and the tendency in some, but not all, modern 'hymns' to be vague in meaning, secular in nature, or possibly with little apparent scriptural base. He questions what a Cambridge church historian and writer on the hymns of Wesley and Watts, would have made of today's frequent poor regard to rhyme and metre? But unlike him, the author believes only religious verse addressed directly to the Father, Son or Holy Spirit can truly be a hymn. If the Bible is accepted as the Word of God, then paraphrase is still Word to our ears. Only when the text is rearranged to form a prayer can paraphrase truly become a hymn. This is not to dismiss other 'hymns' which can touch the heart, proclaim faith or exhort others to closer communion with the Trinity. The author includes both types of verse!

Unlike the early Christians, we are privileged to see with two thousand years perspective, events that for them had only recently occurred. Can we understand more fully, perhaps, Christ's words and actions and indeed the Word of God Himself? If controversy exists, could this be because we choose to deviate from God's natural Law and His Word?

This edition includes as an Appendix a number of additional poems which I had forgotten I had written, some of which show alternative rhyming and the readers can decide which they find most appropriate.

David Smith

CONTENTS

The Poems   *Page No.*

CONTENTS

CONTENTS

The Thoughts and Meditations   *Page No.*

CONTENTS

Snowdrops at Scagglethorpe North Yorkshire

An Anthology of Verse

with

thoughts and Meditations

For the courageous people of Dunblane,
Victims of landmines and injustice,
Children in need,
And all who suffer,
That faith may flower.

I will always be with you and comfort you…

The Poems on pages 71,73,75,77 and 79 were intended originally as an outline for a children's sketch.

The front cover photograph is Mallyan Spout Waterfall, North Yorkshire.

All photographs are copyright of the author.

In compiling the list of references the author has used the Revised English Bible (O.U.P/C.U.P), many passages from which have been the source of inspiration in his compilation of verse.

THE BEGINNING AND THE END

An idyllic setting, - the perfect home in a perfect landscape designed for a perfect being, - set amidst a garden planted by the Creator himself! Nowhere can be seen brick, steel nor even spire to interrupt the view or peep above the blissful blossoms and thorn-free foliage. No weed invades the garden floor bedecked with flowers of every hue. Creation in all its splendour is in direct communion with the Supreme Being and a peaceful river flows to satisfy and complete man's needs.

Reached only by the river of Christ, - man's ultimate home. Reunited in a perfect re-creation, - set beside a river of life. There is no temple. Once more perfection is found in perpetual communion of man with his Maker.

Genesis 2:8-11; 3:8-10 John 6:54
Revelation 21:22 – 22:5

2

RIVERS OF LIFE

In six days, God did plant a garden fair.
His work was good and pleasing to His face.
Like to His image, first of human race
Adam was formed, then Eve, and set in there.
Goodness abound, with blossoms everywhere.
A peaceful river watered every place.
But so soon was mankind to fall from grace, -
To touch forbidden tree of life did dare.
Yet crystal clear, another river flows, -
Water of life, in a new heaven and earth
Where tears shall be such things which no one knows
And men shall be the objects of rebirth.
A river from the side of Christ still flows
And heavenward pointing, pierced hands stretch forth.

Genesis 1:1-3, 24 John 19:32-34
Revelation 21:1-7; 22:1-2

A CHILD'S VIEW

How simply a child sees the world and all that goes on around him or her. The world is so large and full of wonderment as his eyes look up from his lower plane. But even in the sheer delight of childhood and while of tender years, the child perceives that evil has invaded his initial world of security and perfection. Yet one so young does not see the world through rose-coloured spectacles or try to conceal his feelings. He will react to what he sees and hears. He will state the obvious.

But as he grows older and passes through adolescence and into adulthood, such simplicity becomes clouded with experiences and he finds the simple develops into such complexities that his whole lifetime is spent, consciously or otherwise, probing the wonders and nature of God and the reasons for even his own being.

Matthew 18:3

THE DREADFUL FLOOD

As man grew very bad,
God grew very sad.
He said, "I must destroy
Man, woman, girl and boy.

But Noah, he's been good
And served me as he should.

The world makes a din
Over mankind's dreadful sin,
So I'm going to make it rain and rain.
I'm going to make it rain, rain, rain, - and again!"
(The author's son, as a child)

Genesis 6:9 – 7:23 Matthew 24:37 Luke 17:26

MINEFIELDS OF TRANSGRESSION

Eden laid waste! We are mankind, made in the image of the Creator Himself, yet we are witnesses to our own capability of total devastation, mankind's destruction of everything of beauty, the annihilation of every living thing in one moment of cataclysmic contravention of creation's order. Even so, our senseless passion to destroy is not quelled as dusty tracks are mined across a manmade desert of desolation with weapons of detestable destruction of life and limb. Lost is all love for fellow man as mankind positions himself far from the love of God. But across this self-inflicted spiritual wilderness a lone voice is heard to cry and continues to cry out. 'Outlaw the landmines! Prepare a highway for our God!' A few sincere and repentant people start marking out the way, clearing away the stones and rubble with their bare hands. They are quickly joined by many seeking personal gain, then industrial giants seeing easy profit, vying with each other to secure some big contract. 'Be off,' cries the lone voice. 'God would rather breathe life into the stones themselves to construct the highway which will lead to His eternal peace.'

The narrow highway is completed by God Himself across the wasteland of godless intent and signs erected to guide the faithful travellers. The road is soon heavily congested as it is seen to be a shortcut leading to lower overheads and increased profit. Grime churned up by the wheels of juggernauts obscures the signs. A new type of landmine lines the way for the unwary faithful for whom the route was planned, as every step along the way affords attractive sites for the blinding lights of commercial venture and inventive distractions. But the truly faithful press on, clutching the Creator's Highway Code, - a guide understood in every tongue and the pages of which could never be destroyed. They are constantly hooted at or overtaken by many who flaunt the code, ignoring warning lights, believing their own engines are powerful enough to avoid any dangers yet with total disregard to fellow travellers, or their Creator. They may reluctantly feel obliged from time to time to call in for a service before an MOT certificate can be issued enabling them to continue on their reckless, selfish joyride.

Isaiah 40:1-5; 51:3 Matthew 3:8-9; 7:13-14; 15:7-9; 24:35
Mark 1:2-3 Luke 3:4-8 John 1:23; 14:4-6
Ecclesiasticus 32:20-23

6

THE PATHWAY OF LOVE

Let Your face shine upon me, Your Word set me free;
Take the veil from my eyes Lord, so that I may see
All Your promise and blessings which stream from above
And the earth, all around, which is filled with Your love.

You have known of my hope and my trust from the start
And my praises that spring from sincereness of heart;
All Your Word is the music that savours the tongue
As my jubilant heart, ever fills with Your song.

But Lord, what is this veil so obscuring my sight?
Is it envy and falsehood, - not choosing aright?
Take my wilful neglect of Your precepts, my pride;
Take the veil from my eyes, so reveal and so guide.

Lord, I'll treasure Your promise I hold in my heart
And I'll keep to the pathway that You've set apart,
For the pathway of faithfulness leads to above
Where for ever I'll rest and remain in Your love.

Psalm 119:4-7,11,18,29-32,35-38,81,103,135,169-172

I AM UNIQUE

What is the purpose of life?

Such a profound question! But, 'why was I born?'

I may share many thoughts, many actions, many desires, with other members of the human race, but 'I am unique!'

Perhaps just one of my thoughts has never occurred to any other human being since time began. Could I have experienced an unparalleled insight of something hitherto unknown? Have I placed colours on a canvas in such a way as to reveal a picture previously hidden from our imagination or arranged notes in order to form an unheard melody? Have I discovered some distant star or have my researches uncovered a miracle of the human body?

If I make known for the benefit of mankind any unique thought or discovery, then can I answer why was I born?'

Matthew 25:14-15 Romans 12:6

THE UNSEEN FORCE

And was I born to fight and kill my brother?
Is life's ambition to outlive the other?
The throbbing torment wrought of evil mind
Intent on strife and wiping out mankind!

I search around me, falter, yearn for freedom,
For peace and vision of that heavenly kingdom,
But man, with evil thoughts and deeds, I find,
Whose single aim is to destroy mankind.

Mankind: - a family of men made like God;
Sadly fallen; Subject to the angry rod;
Marked with mortal disobedience and blind
To Christ's salvation for God's lost mankind.

Conscience: - unseen forces in creation's plan;
Vital spark, within the soul of selfish man.
Pray that this power may light the sighted blind,
Unite, in peaceful brotherhood, mankind.

Acts 24:16; 2 Corinthians 5:10-11

DEEPLY MOVED

Who is my brother? I rarely see my brother because of the distance involved. Who is my neighbour? I rarely see my neighbours even though they live next door.

Television pictures via satellite are beamed directly into my living room, live from across the world. Are we now part of one global village? Is Ethiopia just around the corner? Could Somalia be on the next street? Are Rwanda and Burundi only down the road? The on-screen pictures are as clear as the flowers I see in my garden through the patio window. But where do these visual-image people actually live? Where are their homes? I see no supermarket where they can buy food or adequate schools for the children. Where are the electricity cables, telephone wires or even a tap to provide water for their daily needs? How do they receive news and entertainment programmes as there are no television aerials or satellite dishes? Have they ever seen how we live here, as our programmes are beamed across the globe? I wonder if they think of us as their neighbours; or brothers? I watch the television news and hear the chimes of Big Ben, but are these pictures also seen in Westminster and indeed the parliaments of other countries in the developed world? But then we like to feel that our conscience is clear with the percentage of aid given. In that other part of the global village it must surely be untrue that literacy is less than one in five and life expectancy is under fifty? Are those emaciated creatures really human beings; made in the likeness of God? Are they really our neighbours? Are they really our brothers? Can we fail to be deeply moved or like Cain are we saying 'Am I my brother's keeper?'

Soon there will be no need for me to leave my home at all. At the touch of a button I can shop at home, do banking on the Internet, watch live sport, play virtual reality games and even participate in television programmes from the comfort of my own armchair. I won't really need to speak to shop assistants, cashiers or work colleagues. Will I then need a neighbour? Will I then need a brother?

Genesis 4:6-10 Matthew 12:46-50 Mark 3:31-35
Luke 10:25-37 1John 4:20-21

DISTANT BROTHERS

Remember we have brothers
Far off in distant lands,
With food so scarce, but few eat,
And some can barely stand.
Yet still they follow Jesus
And thank Him every day.
O help us, Lord, to help them
And show us how we may.

Some children have no parents
And some have lost their home,
Carry with them all they have
Though know not where they roam.
But God alone is Father
To children, everywhere.
A heavenly home He gives us,
And all shall love Him there.

But whether we have plenty
Or whether we have naught,
With all the gifts God gives us
And all the love Christ brought,
Can each to distant brothers
Far off across the sea,
Offer much in Christ-taught way
And so, Lord, honour Thee.

*Job 29:11-16 1Corinthians 16:1-2 Galatians 2:10
James 1:27*

DAY-BREAK

I was so, so tired last night. My head just touched the pillow and, - I never heard another sound. I slept really well. I feel so refreshed!

Just listen to the birds. Can you hear the robin? What a lovely song! It's such a beautiful morning. Draw back the curtains. Oh, I love the sun streaming through like that. Isn't everything simply wonderful!

This beautiful new dawn I now know is a gift from God. A new Day! I will cast aside all those futile worries of yesterday, the misjudged grievances I had against those I should love and the disappointments I failed to recognise as blessings. Today I will truly love you, Lord.

Exodus 16:6-7 Psalm 30:4-5; 59:16 Isaiah 50:4

THIS NEW DAY

This new day Lord, I will live for You, -
Loving ways pursue, - do Your will.
This new day Lord, I will live for You.
Love anew. Yes, I will.

Each new day Lord, I will live with You, -
Earthly thoughts subdue, - do Your will.
Each new day Lord, I will live with You.
Be with You. Yes, I will.

Genesis 28:11,16 Psalm 145:1-2

STARTING SCHOOL

I remember very clearly my first day at school. In those days you had to have reached the age of five even to be considered being accepted for a place. Classes were large and our numbers reached in excess of fifty before leaving Junior School. Only the week before starting school it seemed I had still actually been clinging to my mother's apron strings. This had indeed happened every time the air-raid siren sounded. I did not know what my father looked like. He was away in India but I was never told. I did not know of war or even violence, yet instinctively the wail of the sirens had struck fear right through me.

I had left my mother at the school gates where she looked on anxiously with a group of other mothers whilst the teacher took me by the hand and led me through the imposing school entrance doors and into a lofty classroom. She asked me my name and then wrote it on a card and my first task was to practice writing it. How important that first assignment has proved to be over the years! It was the first time I think I had ever seen my name written. Playtime was a joy when we all had a milk break. We each took a small bottle from a huge milk crate, a straw from a box simply crammed full of them, pushed it through the cardboard milk bottle top, and revitalised our tired bodies.

When it was time to go home, we all sang 'Thank you for the world so sweet, thank you for the food we eat, thank you for the birds that sing, thank you God for everything. Amen.' Then we all lifted our chairs onto our desktops so that the floor was clear for the caretaker to come in and sweep the room clean ready for the next day. Furthest from our minds was that schooling was to prepare us for the outside world and future work to earn our livings to support our families, or the many selfish ways we each would go about taking care of ourselves with hardly a thought for others.

Ephesians 5:19-20

LOVE, FLOW THROUGH ME

Open our eyes to see Your love
Descending on us from above; -
Our blindness clear and stumbling cease
In visions of Your heavenly peace.

Open our hearts; - forgive our sin, -
And let Your loveliness flow in.
Your kindly mercies then impart
To each receptive, thankful, heart.

Open our minds, our conscience clear, -
Our every thought of You hold dear,
In steadfast confidence to find
True faith and fortitude of mind.

Open our ears, Your word to hear, -
Truths which the Advocate makes clear,
And giving heed, Lord, to Your will,
Love others, as You love us still.

Close our desire for self and gain, -
An egoistic cause of pain.
So may we shun all wrong and ill,
And always seek to do Your will.

1Corinthians 2:9; 13:4-7; 2Corinthians 3:14-16,18; 4:6

TONGUES

The tongue seems to me one part of the body you take for granted as a child. You naturally learn to speak. You don't think to yourself, I must waggle my tongue and say a few words today! You know that sweets taste good and ice cream is delicious without giving the tongue a thought. It may not be until you come across some less fortunate person with a lisp or who is tongue-tied that you realise how important your tongue is.

Perhaps when you grow older you decide to learn to play a musical instrument and choose, say, a flute or the oboe. You soon discover then how much more there is to the tongue and how difficult it can be to train it to respond exactly how you would wish, but when you have mastered tonguing techniques you are able to appreciate the beautiful sounds the tongue can help to create.

But I'm sure there was a time when someone pointed their tongue at you or, worse still, you stuck out your tongue at them. All too soon, we learn that the tongue can be used in anger, for abuse, for gossiping and for telling lies. The tongue, despite its size, can be the most wicked part of the body. But the tongue is also the means by which we need never let sunset find us still nursing our anger.

Psalm 34:13-14; 52:1-4,8-9 Proverbs 10:20
Ephesians 4:26

TRUE TO YOU

How can I but proclaim Your love,
When all around I see
The beauty of Your handiwork
Created, Lord, for me?

The sun and moon in silence move
Across the noiseless sky,
Yet Lord, through them, Your voice is clear
If we use ear and eye.

From day to day and night to night
Your light upon me shines.
I cannot flee from sun or moon
Or hide from Your designs.

Your perfect law revives my soul, -
Refocuses my eyes.
Your teachings never fail me, Lord,
But make the simple wise.

As honey dripping from the comb,
Your blessings are more sweet.
More precious than the purest gold
Are prayers before Your feet.

My wilful sins I here confess,
Forgiving Lord, to You.
But cleanse me too of all the wrong,
Unwittingly, I do.

May all my words and all my thoughts
In everything be true,
As with a joyful, willing, heart
Your precepts I pursue.

As in the heavens and on the earth
Your glories, Lord, I view,
May all my paling actions, be
Acceptable to You?

Psalm 19

WORD PICTURE

In the beginning was the Word, and the Word was with God. But the Word was made flesh, and blood, and bones, - human flesh and blood, born like us, born for us, and came to live with us. The Word became a living, breathing, enactment. Each scene of life became a living word picture, - the Master's own Word-painting.

All the great masters in art gave substance to their work. They used the brightest colours to contrast sharply with the darkest shadows. Black was used alongside gold. Hidden meanings were often concealed in contrasting images, the subtle use of light and darkness, but the finished painting had a completeness all its own. A wholeness shone through bringing the picture to life.

God has given His Word to us, but just as the artist takes up the colours from his palette, arranging them on the canvas with differing strokes of the brush in order to express his emotions, so we are given the gifts of thought and expression to arrange words in such ways as new or previously hidden meanings can be revealed in the stories of old.

John 1:1-5 Ephesians 3:7-12 Colossians 1:25-27

HOPE OF THE WORLD

Jesus, asleep in a manger of hay, -
Hope of the world, born of Mary this day.
Jostling crowds throng the innkeeper's hall,
Quite unaware of the Babe in the stall.

Shepherds keep watch on a mountain nearby.
Black is the night, then one star fills the sky.
Angels above sing 'A new Lamb is born!
Come; see the Lamb of God. Welcome His dawn.'

Seers on a journey bear gold for a King.
Incense and myrrh, with their treasures, they bring.
Bethlehem beckons. A dark stable room
Heralds a Kingdom, - yet foretells a tomb.

Prophesies, old, long-forgotten but true:
God's love, - His plan for mankind to renew.
His Son, asleep in a manger of hay; -
Hope of the world, born of Mary this day.

Isaiah 42:8-9 Matthew 2:1-2,11 Luke 2:7-14
Ephesians 1:3-10 Colossians 1:27

TELL ME A STORY

How I remember with such delight those bedtimes when the children were young. Arms were tired and legs weary as each day was filled with new adventure and play, yet minds were still so alert as you tucked them into bed. 'Tell us that story again, dad. Please.'

There was no story if truth were told. In any case they were nonsense stories really. The first thing that came into my head was turned into some magical adventure that captivated the children's attention. You were urged to continue the story although you knew neither where it was going nor how it could end. Yet what wonderful adventures they turned out to be!

But best of all were the Christmas Eves, climbing the stairs together singing as we went, clutching the stockings to hang by their pillows. As parents, secretly knowing what gifts the children would wake to receive on Christmas Morning. Then a special Christmas lullaby composed spontaneously but perhaps mindful of that moment shortly to arrive after the bedtime story was over when you would tiptoe softly across the bedroom floor after tired eyes had at last closed in slumber.

But what of our heavenly Father's gifts for us? How excitedly does He, and should we, anticipate the morrow?

Matthew 7:11 Luke 11:13

THE CHILDREN VISIT THE STABLE

Enter, shepherd boy.
Quietly peep at Jesus.
Place your woolly toy
By the side of Jesus.
Softly tiptoe, through the darkened stable.
Gently, gently rock the baby's cradle.

Come near, shepherdess.
Hold the baby Jesus.
Lovingly caress
Tiny Saviour, -Jesus.
Softly tiptoe, through the darkened stable.
Gently, gently rock the baby's cradle.

Hurry, wise man's son,
'Till your star finds Jesus.
Spur your camel on
To discover Jesus.
Softly tiptoe, through the darkened stable.
Gently, gently rock the baby's cradle.

Fear not, little maid.
Leave your inn, for Jesus.
Do not be afraid
Now to serve dear Jesus.
Softly tiptoe, through the darkened stable.
Gently, gently rock the baby's cradle.

Matthew 2:9-11 Luke 2:15-18

SUPREMELY HAPPY

Do you remember a time when you were supremely happy?

Take a look through 'Baby's Own Book,' – the record of the birth of your own child! Read the details you lovingly recorded of the date, and place, and time, when baby waved goodbye to the stork! See the weight, the height, and the colour of the eyes, all written down with pride. Look at the first lock of hair carefully preserved and feel the memories flooding back of that supremely happy time. Yet the baby knew nothing of the joy his birth brought to the parents, grandparents, uncles and aunts, or even, perhaps, to older brothers and sisters.

Jesus once stood on a hillside overlooking the beautiful Sea of Galilee. He addressed the crowd that had followed him, eager to hear him teach. They were deeply unhappy with their lives and the situation in which they found themselves and their nation. These are the ways he told them they would find true happiness if they knew they were spiritually poor: -
    If they were in mourning,
    If they were meek,
    If their greatest wish was to do what God required,
    If they showed mercy to others,
    If they were pure in heart,
    If they worked for peace,
    If they suffered in doing God's will,
    If they were insulted, mistreated, and the object of
evil lies because they followed him.

In this way, they would be 'Beatitudo' – supremely happy.

Matthew 5:1-11

THE LONG-AWAITED KING

Glad tidings sing, to one and all,
Upon this joyous day; -
A new-born child, so still and small,
Is cradled in the hay.
    High in heaven above
    Angels sing of love,
    For the Christ-child's born today.
    Yet the King of Love
    Left His home above; -
    Christ, be born in us we pray.

A king of Truth and Righteousness
Is born beneath a star,
And fills our hearts with happiness
Though we be near or far.
    High in heaven above
    Angels sing of love,
    For the Christ-child's born today.
    Yet the King of Love
    Left His home above; -
    Christ, be born in us we pray.

O righteous King, lowly and meek, -
And yet You are so strong,
You are the King of Kings we seek, -
For whom we've waited long.
    High in heaven above
    Angels sing of love,
    For the Christ-child's born today.
    Yet the King of Love
    Left His home above; -
    Christ, be born in us we pray.

Glad tidings sing. This new-born king,
So snuggled in the hay,
He is the gift of peace and hope,
And love, this Christmas Day.

Matthew 2:1-2,9-11 Luke 2:6-14 John 6:38-40

THE A-Z OF MIRACLES

An A-Z of miracles! Lord, you chose to perform your first miracle at a wedding. The Alpha of your miraculous powers stunned the onlookers who marvelled with astonishment. You chose a time when the joining of a man and a woman in marriage manifested human love, and when families and friends met together, united in their love for the happy couple.

The Omega! We eagerly await the final miracle for which you have chosen another wedding, - the marriage of Christ to His Church, - when families and friends will again be united in love for the Godhead. At that time, the waters of the river flowing through the New Holy City will be given life-giving power and the leaves of trees along it's banks be given healing property.

But sadly, for a variety of reasons, so often marriage vows prove impossible to keep. When Abram arrived in Canaan with his nephew Lot, the land was unable to support them both, so they reached an agreement to take separate areas. Later, Abram became Abraham on entering into a covenant with God. At any time if they so chose, Abram and Lot could have rescinded or revised their agreement by mutual consent. But Christ established a new covenant with God to bring liberation from sins committed under Abraham's earlier covenant.

Could a couple, therefore, be free to revoke a civil agreement by mutual consent, but if they find they are unable to fulfil the vows they have made before God, should not they alone come to lay their case before God and seek His guidance, agreement and blessing of the course of action they ultimately decide?

Genesis 13:8-12; 17:4-10 John 2:1-11 Hebrews 8:7-13
Revelation 21:1-6; 22:1-2

24

THE WEDDING STORY

Into Your house, we come with joy and gladness
Eager for You to meet the one we love.
Come, loving Lord, come with Your loving kindness, -
Come and perfect and purify our love.

Be with us Lord, as we kneel with each other
Seeking Your blessing on our wedding day.
Your loving presence may we know and ever
Love each as You have loved us, so we pray.

As first in Cana You revealed Your glory
When turning water into choicest wine,
This joyful day renew the wedding story
Turning our hearts, perfect our love like Thine.

May our love grow with patience and with kindness
As we together start our married life,
Led by the Spirit, guided to Your likeness,
Until our loves unite in heaven's pure life.

John 2:1-11; 15:8-12 1Corinthians 13:4-13

WHAT'S IN A WORD?

Take time. God is in no hurry. He listens to our every word. But how often we cut short our prayer to him as we try to cram everything into our busy schedules. Our prayers become rapid, repetitious, ritual renditions. How tiresome for God! In our haste, or our need to keep to strict timetables, we sometimes deliberately cut them short. In such ways we falsely give ourselves the sense of fulfilling our obligations to God.

But how did Jesus teach us to pray? He made it sound so simple, and simple it really is, but what's in a word? 'Our Father, which art in heaven.' 'Heaven?' 'Father?' Even 'our'. What's in a word? Examine each word or phrase. Can we truthfully say this word or that phrase to God today? Perhaps, after all, it is sometimes better to omit a phrase or cut short a prayer and leave it unsaid until the morrow or some other day when we can approach God and confess or give thanks to Him with a truthful heart.

But Jesus taught us what to say before He died for us, before He rose to conquer death and before He ascended to reign with the Father in glory. He listens to our every word with the Father in heaven.

What's in a word? God hears every one.

Psalm 65:2 John 14:12-14

HOW TO PRAY

Father in heaven, and Father of Jesus Christ our Lord,
        With You in heaven,
Let Your Name be reverenced throughout Your earthly kingdom
        Just as in heaven.

Strengthen us daily by Your Spirit.

You have forgiven us all our wrongdoing through Your Son.
May we learn to forgive others to the same extent.
        Enable us to avoid temptation
        So that good may overcome evil
And establish forever Your Kingdom on this earth
Where all glory, and majesty, and power, is Yours.

Matthew 6:9-13 Luke 11:2-4

27

CHOSEN TO STAY

Moses! Moses! I need you to lead my people from their bondage. Please not me cries Moses. It's no good asking me, I'm too slow. You'll be much better off asking someone else. In any case, I'm not a very good persuader, so no one will take any notice of what I say. Leave me alone. I'm happy as I am. I'd rather wander for forty years through the wilderness than do as you ask!

Jonah! Jonah! I need you to go to Ninevah and denounce its wickedness. Why ask me cries Jonah. Send someone else. In fact, I'd rather face a mighty storm, be shipwrecked, or even be swallowed up in the belly of a whale than do what you ask! Please find someone else to go.

Job! Job! I need your family and I need all your possessions. I need them now, this very minute. But surely not mine cries Job. You know I've never caused anyone any pain or suffering. I haven't hurt or injured anybody. I wouldn't hurt a fly. I've tried my utmost to live a good and honest life and never doubted your greatness. Why must you do this to me? I would rather I had never been born if you're going to treat me like this!

Job! Answer me just this one question. Which is the most important, that I decide to take to myself that which is already mine, or choose to leave you behind because there is a purpose to the life I have given you, and I have a purpose to fulfil?

Exodus 3:4 – 4:13: Job: Jonah 1:1-3

THE SNOWDROPS OF DUNBLANE

Did snowdrops grow in Galilee
Two thousand years ago,
Or Jesus, on a mountain-top,
Leave footprints in the snow; -
And did a child bring snowdrops sweet,
And place them in His hand; -
And when He blessed the children, did
The people understand?

Save the children. Love the children.
Let them come, as to His knee.
Save the children. Love the children.
Bless them. Hug them tenderly.

Did Jesus walk upon these hills
And vales, in this our land,
And did He see the snowdrops that
Grow here at God's command; -
And did He take them in His hands
And bless their colours bright; -
The green for youth's fresh energies, -
Pure children's hearts -the white?

Save the children. Love the children.
Let them come, as to His knee.
Save the children. Love the children.
Bless them. Hug them tenderly.

Each year when we're reminded by
The snowdrops and the snow,
Give thanks for little lives that here
And in God's garden grow,
Assured that, as the spring precedes
The summer, we shall see
Our children with their snowdrops, still
Alive round Jesu's knee.

Matthew 19:13-15 Mark 9:36-37; 13:24-33

PELICAN CROSSING

Look right. Look left. Then look right again and cross only if it's clear. That's how we were taught to cross the road when we were young. Then came the Belisha beacon, an amber-coloured globe erected on the pavement where officially it was considered safe to cross. A space probe had left our universe before ever I knew Belisha was the Minister of Transport! We then had the Zebra and this was followed by a Pelican Crossing. It sounds a bit like Noah leading the animals across a busy road in order to reach the ark! The interesting thing about the Pelican Crossing is that not only do you see the flashing light but you hear a warning signal. We are taught to use both ear and eye.

Jesus often taught the people by parables. They had to listen, but he asked them to observe what was happening around them. 'Watch the sower! Look at all the places where the seed falls. See how different ground results in differing levels of growth. If you look and listen and understand, then you will have been given the secret of the kingdom of God. But you look and look yet see nothing; you listen and listen but fail to understand. When you see the fig tree's tender shoots appear and break into leaf you know that summer is very near. Be on your guard and watch for the signs of the coming of the Son of Man in the clouds with great power and glory.'

Genesis 7:1-9 Matthew 13:3,10-17 Mark 4:3-12
Luke 8:5-9

SPRING

GREEN LEAVES: hid through long winter's night
From tightened bud, burst into view.
In spring, our God has set a sight
Of pastel green, and tender hue.

SPRING FLOWERS: as now their colours peep
Through hardened earth or glist'ning snow,
And petals peer, when they from sleep
Awake. They give a glad'ning show.

YOUNG LAMBS: before the snows give way
To pleasant fields and blossom tree,
In meadows sweet, they frisk and play
With careless skip, and frolic free.

NEW LIFE: through Christ we have rebirth
Then grow, in love, yet here to die
A mortal death upon this earth,
But to aspire to life on high.

Psalm 114:4,6-8 Isaiah 61:11 Mark 13:28 John 3:16

SURELY NOT A SHEEP

How simply great it is to be out walking in the countryside on a glorious summer's day. Far from the hustle and bustle of the city and choking fumes, how wonderful to breathe in the pure air, hear the song of the birds, let your eyes wander over endless views of fields and hills, and watch the ever-changing skies. It's so easy there to feel close to God in nature.

But surely I'm not one of those sheep! Do I really look and act like one of those silly creatures? Well, Psalm 23 seems to suggest I may be. The Lord is 'my' shepherd. So if I'm not a sheep then what does it mean? A staff and a crook comfort me! Ask any child if they would like a few strokes of the cane and whether that would be comforting. Then what's this table doing out in the middle of the countryside, - and set for a sheep? I've heard of the teddy-bears picnic but this is really over the top!

But I know there was once a table set for you Lord and you were betrayed by one of your friends who left before the meal was finished. And I know you keep setting a table for me Lord, in an undeserving world. You certainly know me or you wouldn't keep doing it.

I think you're more a guide, Lord. A guide cannot guide those he doesn't know; otherwise he wouldn't know if they were missing.

Psalm 23 Matthew 26: 20-29 Mark 14:18-24
Luke 22:14-23 John 13:21-30

THE TABLES OF OUR LORD

Lord, when You saw the shepherds on
The hills of Galilee,
Or rested in those pastures green
Beside a spangled sea,
You knew Your Father walked with You,
As shepherds with their sheep,
But never feared the dark to come,
For God, His watch would keep.

Then when You reached that Upper Room
And saw the table spread,
You knew one would betray and flee,
But when You shared the bread,
As God's anointed, did not flinch
To face faith's final test,
Assured that You would overcome
And in God's presence, rest.

You know me, Lord, for You're my guide
And nothing else I need,
As to the water-spring of God
Your words, my spirit, lead.
You guide my earthly progress, Lord,
Throughout the darkest day.
Why should I fear, when this I know, -
That You have passed this way?

And when I see Your table spread
With bread and wine for me,
But set for all, amidst a world
Of hate and poverty,
May I, with thanks, recall the price
You paid, that I might live
To share with You, the place within
Your home, to me, You give?

Psalm 23 Matthew 26:20-29,36-39 Mark 14:18-24,32-36
Luke 22:14-23,39-46 John 14:2-3

33

JERUSALEM VALETE

On my first visit to Israel, on the 'plane I sat next to an artist and writer. During the flight we shared much of our common interests and exchanged small tokens of our work. He was sure I could not fail to be moved or receive fresh insight by some of the sights I would see in the Holy Land.

On my return I thought long and hard about this. In particular, I found I was able to relate sounds and sights with descriptions of events noted in the Bible and place the spoken words that are recorded in context. But what of the unspoken thoughts of people, which the gospel writers could not know?

'Father, here on the Mount of Olives, above Gethsemane, I stand ready to return to You. You have indeed accepted me as the only perfect sacrifice in settlement of this world's wickedness. Just as You promised, and I believed, I have passed through death and I bring to You Your own. As I turn and look back over Your chosen city, I can see the spot where I was betrayed, the place where I was tried, and the mound where they crucified me. Did it really have to be like this? I can see where in years gone by, Your purposes first began to be fulfilled. I see the temple upon the rock where Abraham himself was about to sacrifice his son, Isaac, yet You provided him with a replacement sacrifice. But Father, I have indeed been faithful to Your purposes. There was no other way: it had to be.'

Genesis 22:1-14 Acts 1:9

ON CHRIST'S ASCENSION

O quiet Kidron, could you not collect my countless tears
  As over yonder Zion's Mount I wept?
Could you not flood with bloodstained beads from off my burning brow
  And barrier build between betrayer's kiss?
O mighty stones, firm on Foundation's Rock, and fortress walls,
  Why could you not collapse as traitor crept
Close by your buttress walls? Why wait awhile for future fall?
  O olive, rooted by the hecklers' hiss, -
Gethsemane forsook, - for grim Golgotha's gruesome gaze!
  Forlorn your fruit and oil, - why nails accept?

'Twas I who chose the bitter cup as here I knelt in prayer.
  'Wait Golden Gate, my Coming Genesis!

Matthew 23:37 – 24:2; 26:36-46 Mark 13:1-2; 14:32-42
Luke 13:34-35; 22:39-48 Revelation 22:12-13

STILL GAZING

I visited one of our great cathedrals between Good Friday and Easter Day. Inside I found a beautiful tableau, a representation of the Garden Tomb. There was a garden to the fore, with flowers and shrubs and a pathway, and the tomb was hewn into a small hillside. Three crosses stood on a hillside in the background. Criminals hung on the outer crosses but the centre cross stood empty. A large rounded stone, like a giant wheel, sealed the entrance to the tomb. I was unable to return the following day when I am sure I would have found the same display but with the stone rolled to one side revealing an empty tomb.

I was reminded of an earlier visit to Jerusalem where I walked the Via Dolorosa, the Way of the Cross, I entered the Church of the Holy Sepulchre, stepped into the empty tomb, and also visited the Garden Tomb a short distance away. Everywhere people stood and gazed, just as they did two thousand years ago.

Have you seen the place? Have you seen the stone? Have you stood and gazed? Are we still, perhaps, just gazing?

Matthew 13:13-14 Hebrews 10:32-33

YOU WILL SEE ME

Come; see the place where our Lord lay.
He is not here, but risen today.
God's angel rolled the stone away.
       Hallelujah!

Seek you the Lord? Then have no fear.
Your risen Saviour will appear.
The living Christ is ever near.
       Hallelujah!

The third day saw the Saviour rise, -
Soon to ascend beyond the skies, -
The Son of Man, hid from our eyes.
       Hallelujah!

Men of this world, - why stand and gaze?
Through all the earth Christ's witness raise,
'Till earth and heaven are joined in praise.
       Hallelujah!

Matthew 28:5-7 Mark 16:2-7 Luke 24:1-7 Acts 1:9-11

GRATEFULNESS

Do you find that so often when you have deliberately gone out of your way to show an act of kindness or assistance that you seem to receive absolutely no thanks whatsoever? It's not that you were expecting a word of thanks and certainly not seeking any reward but, after all, it costs nothing to say 'thank you.' But then there are times when you did something, so small it seemed, and you are quite overwhelmed by the reaction and cannot justify receiving presents, thank-you cards and embarrassing praise in return.

When something is given gratuitously, it is freely bestowed or freely obtained. It costs the recipient absolutely nothing and is given without good ground or reason. How dubious we are of any free gift in a world of sales gimmickry where we consider nothing to be given free any more with no strings attached.

The psalmist said 'I shall always go on singing of the loving deeds of the Lord.' Paul, in his letter to Timothy, shows how he is enthused and inspired by the gift by God of His Son to us, and the gift by Christ of His life for us. 'I am not ashamed of this good news,' he proclaims, 'for I have been appointed its herald, apostle and teacher.'

I shall go on rejoicing, for the Spirit of Jesus Christ is given me for support.

Psalm 89:1 2Timothy 1:6-14

THANK YOU, LORD

I thank my God, who sent His Son for me,
To die that awful death, at Calvary.
The Father knew it was the only way
For our salvation. Through His Son, we may
        To God return.

I thank my Saviour that He took my place
Convicted, though of sin He had no trace.
The cross and cruel nails were meant for me
As chief offender, yet He set me free
        By dying there.

I thank the Holy Spirit for the power
And strength I find in every passing hour,
My peace and comfort that is always near,
My constant guide and help, and teacher dear,
        And joy to prove.

I thank my Maker for the love He shows.
His truth is near. His light within me glows
So bright that all His praises I must tell
Until all round me know my Christ as well
        As now I know.

Psalm 16:8-11 Acts 2:22-36,39

BREAKING OUT

I'm what you might call an armchair snooker player. I like to watch a good break. A break is actually the point at which a series of successful strokes comes to an end. The continuity of play is broken.

'Peace has broken out.' How I hate to hear that expression, often used in news reports. War may break out, but when hostilities cease does peace really 'break out'? Peace is freedom from war or hostilities. It is the time when nations or communities are not waging war or, for the individual, when there is no mental or spiritual disturbance. To break out implies force, an act of violence, but peace is gentle and cannot be forced. It seems more likely that peace has to be allowed to find its way in for war to cease. A peacemaker brings about that cessation by reconciling the opposing factions.

Jesus described the peacemakers as 'blessed,' endowed with virtue and the favour of God. 'The peace which I have, I'm leaving with you,' he said. He didn't say 'I'm leaving my peace in you.' It would seem, therefore, that we have to allow his peace to find its way in. Then we have 'inner' peace.

Matthew 5:9 John 14:27

INNER PEACE

I feel Your inner peace, Lord, - I feel Your peace.
I feel Your inner peace, Lord, - I feel Your peace.
    Safe, safe within Your loving arms I rest,
    Sure, that with heaven's grace I'm blest.
I feel Your inner peace, Lord, - I feel Your peace.

I know You hear my prayer, Lord, - You hear my prayer.
I know You hear my prayer, Lord, - You hear my prayer.
    Thanks, thanks for all the care and love You show:
    I know You paid the debt I owe.
I know You hear my prayer, Lord, - You hear my prayer.

I feel Your hand in mine, Lord, - I feel Your hand.
I feel Your hand in mine, Lord, - I feel Your hand.
    Glad, glad that You now walk and talk with me,
    Sure that one day Your face I'll see, -
I feel Your hand in mine, Lord, - I feel Your hand.

I know the Spirit's strength, Lord, - the Spirit's strength.
I know the Spirit's strength, Lord, - the Spirit's strength.
    Joy, joy, I have no doubting heart or fear,
    Sure of Your presence always near.
I know the Spirit's strength, Lord, - the Spirit's strength.

I feel Your inner peace, Lord, - I feel Your peace.
I feel Your inner peace, Lord, - I feel Your peace.
    Safe, safe within Your loving arms I rest,
    Sure that with heaven's grace I'm blest.
I feel Your inner peace, Lord, - I feel Your peace.

Isaiah 41:10 John 14:25-27 Romans 15:13
Hebrews 4:14-16

GENESIS

Right at the very beginning, the Word was there and the Word was with God. It's such a beautiful passage, the opening verses of the good news recorded by St. John in his gospel. Perhaps, like me, you have read or listened to these words without fully understanding them. Shall we ever really know the true creation story? Never mind. What is true is that God and the Word know and were there, and the Word became flesh, was born, like us, and came to live among us.

So Jesus was and is the Word, then? He was there in the beginning, at creation, with God, even when all was darkness and everything was without form? I suppose, then, that the Holy Spirit must also have been there? In the account of creation, I remember it does say that the Spirit moved over the waters. It all makes sense, then, - 'Three in One.' If God was only One in the beginning, He wouldn't suddenly become Three, would He? And if He lit up the darkness, that's clear! Isn't it?

Genesis 1:1-5 John 1:1-14

ACCEPT US, LORD

Light: unmastered by the darkness.
Word: with God, - experienced now.
Sp rit: sprinkle heaven's goodness
As in prayer, our heads, we bow.
Heavenly gift: rebuffed by heartless
Piercing of the Saviour's brow.
Crucified, You proved our weakness.
Glorified, accept us now.

Cause Your face to shine upon us.
As our prayers ascend above
To the source of grace and kindness.
Save and bless us with Your love.

Light: unmastered by the darkness.
Word: with God, - experienced now.
Spirit: sprinkle heaven's goodness
As in prayer, our heads, we bow.
Heavenly gift: rebuffed by heartless
Piercing of the Saviour's brow.
Crucified, You proved our weakness.
Glorified, accept us now.

Sanctify and keep us holy,
That we may mature to know,
Taste, and touch Your love and goodness
As in faith and hope we grow.

Light: unmastered by the darkness.
Word: with God, - experienced now.
Spirit: sprinkle heaven's goodness
As in prayer, our heads, we bow.
Heavenly gift: rebuffed by heartless
Piercing of the Saviour's brow.
Crucified, You proved our weakness.
Glorified, accept us now.

Hear the firstborn shout in triumph.
Earth rejoices. God sustains.
By His Word, made flesh, His greatness
Purges us of all our stains.

Light: unmastered by the darkness.
Word: with God, - experienced now.
Spirit: sprinkle heaven's goodness
As in prayer, our heads, we bow.
Heavenly gift: rebuffed my heartless
Piercing of the Saviour's brow.
Crucified, You proved our weakness.
Glorified, accept us now.

God, be gracious still toward us.
May Your purposes be plain.
Hear Your people's praise and witness,-
Witness to our Saviour's reign.

Light: unmastered by the darkness.
Word: with God,- experienced now.
Spirit: sprinkle heaven's goodness
As in prayer, our heads, we bow.
Heavenly gift: rebuffed by heartless
Piercing of the Saviour's brow.
Crucified, You proved our weakness.
Glorified, accept us now.

Psalm 67 John 1:1-5 Hebrews 6:1-6

MAKE US GROW

Father, we all are Your garden. We are not just one kind of plant but a variety of every conceivable form of flower, tree and shrub. Water us, and make us all grow to perfection in Your garden. Some of us have strong stalks, others the most delicate petals. You have planted Your garden on a fertile plain, and surrounded it by mountains and hills to protect it from destructive winds.

You have planted Your church with children of every colour, race and nation, and set leaders, teachers and protectors over it. Water Your church with Your Spirit and make it grow, enabling each member to perform the particular task to which You have assigned them. Raise spirits, make eyes sparkle, give healing, life and blessing. You hear even the silent prayer, but not if hearts are cold and unforgiving. Amazing things happen when we pray to You in faith, Lord. You have said that we should keep on praying and never lose heart.

Isaiah 51:3; 58:11 Jeremiah 31:12
1Corinthians 12:4-11, 27-28

HEARER OF PRAYER

Hearer of prayer, we praise You now
In Zion's halls above.
From east and west, we sing aloud
The triumph of Your love.
Grant us the bounty of Your house,
The temple courts, our home,
Trusting Your strong deliv'ring power
As we approach Your throne.

Chooser of man, with thankful hearts
Abundantly forgiven,
To farthest shore all praise Your Name
Who glimpse Your glorious heaven.
Delivered from this mindless world
And roaring nations' wrong,
Your sign, with awe, uplifts the soul
To new, more worthy, song.

Fount of our faith, Your mighty hand
Ordains Your church below.
Your Spirit channels, waters, feeds,
As fruitfully we grow,
Restored to You, by sacrifice,
Recalled through bread and wine.
Unblemished may Your harvest be.
Your crown upon us shine.

Psalm 65 Revelation 14:14-16

BLINDNESS

How I love John Milton's poem, his sonnet 'On his blindness.' If I were to compile my 'top ten' in poetry, it would probably head the list. Amazingly he composed it when he was in despair because he went blind at a time he believed he was not even half way through his life's work. In his sonnet, at first he is quite bitter about his predicament but then he has the realisation of just how God works and how man is able to respond to even the most personal of tragedies.

It's strange how Saul also was blinded on the Damascus Road. At the time, he too thought he was at the height of his career and achievement.

John 9:3-5, 39-41 Acts 9:1-9

ST. PAUL

By human birth, I am a Jew; a man named Saul.
Proud of my God, my sign, my knowledge of His law;
My heritage, - the chosen race! What need of more
Than zealous deeds to guard the faith? Such was my call
To persecute, arrest and bring about their fall,
Disciples of a new High Priest, proclaimed the door
To God Himself! Heaven! - For the gentile, sinner, poor?
They claimed this Christ be risen from the dead! But Paul
Is my new name, since blinded by a flash of light
As travelling on Damascus Road, the Lord Himself
Redeemed me through His boundless grace, but first my sight
Denied. In darkness, like His tomb, I dwelt myself
For three, long nights. Now, boldly with His Spirit's might,
I, to all nations, bring the grace of God Himself!

Acts 21:37 – 22:15

47

TRIANGLES

At our morning assembly in junior school we received a gentle introduction to classical music. Once a week, a teacher would play a favourite gramophone record, - 78rpm of course, so listening to the whole piece lasted no more than about four minutes on a 12-inch record. We also had 'band' practice when various percussion instruments, which were kept in a large cupboard in the corner of the classroom, were handed out to the pupils. Possibly because of the great music we had listened to in assembly, I always felt most dejected when I ended up with a triangle. I was most privileged if I was lucky enough to get the castanets!

Could this early involvement with the triangle have been responsible for geometry being my best subject when it came to mathematics? And so the right-angled triangle led me to the square on the hypotenuse and Pythagoras and on to a love of the Greek islands and Samos in particular, the birthplace of Pythagoras!

Our relationship with God, perhaps, is like a triangle. We stand on earth at the very tip of the right-angle. God in His heaven is in the square on the hypotenuse. On one of the other sides, Jesus stretches out between the Father, and us and on the remaining side, the Holy Spirit pours down to us. The triangle is thus complete and unbroken. It starts and ends with God, and God is Love.

John 20:19-22 Romans 14:17-18
2Corinthians 13:14

LOVE! TRUTH!

LOVE!
Love is my Lord.
Love is the Lord, Almighty God.
LOVE.
God is Love!
You are my Lord.
My Lord God is LOVE!

TRUTH!
Truth is my Lord.
Truth is the Lord, Almighty God.
TRUTH.
God is Truth!
You are my Lord.
My Lord God is TRUTH!

LOVE!
Love is my Lord.
Love is the Lord, Almighty God.
LOVE.
God is Love!
You are my Lord.
My Lord God is LOVE!

Exodus 34:6 Psalm 40:10-11

HOLD TIGHT MI DUCKS!

It seems quite a modern idea to have buses with the door at the front. It's easy for the driver to collect the fares, isn't it? When I was young all the latest buses had the door at the back, - well, not really a door exactly, merely an open platform to stand on with a vertical pole to hold on tight to. I think they must have been designed to help those people who were always late for work so they could jump on board after the bus had moved off! But there were still some of the old buses running at that time which had the door at the front. Bone-shakers we called them because they had hard, wooden, slatted seats. The driver didn't collect the fares in those days; his job was to drive the bus. The bus conductor took the money. He had his peaked cap, clutched his ticket holder which held coloured tickets secured by metal springs, a different colour for each priced fare, and his ticket puncher fixed to a leather strap round his shoulder. A little bell sounded as each ticket was clipped. My favourite conductor, however, felt he had additional duties to perform, namely to entertain the passengers with his jokes and comments on the issues of the day, as well as assist little old ladies onto the bus. 'Come on mi ducks,' he would say, 'wi won't go wi 'owt yer.'

Mi ducks! I was surprised to find in later life this really is a true meaning for a charming or delightful person, whilst checking the dictionary definition of love. We all loved that conductor and he loved all the passengers, not only just the little old ladies. He certainly loved that old bone-shaker!

The dictionary told me that love is a feeling of warm attraction, or a kindly act. Love is feelings of devotion and fidelity between male and female. It is to hold dear and it is God's goodness to us and our devotion to Him.

John 3:16 Romans 5:6-11

CAN WE BE CALLED CHRISTIAN?

Can love be so impatient:
Be real, if unkind:
And what if love seems envious,
Or heedless of mankind?

Can love be rude and selfish
Or quick to take offence;
Conceited, gloating, thoughtless,
And full of arrogance?

Does love see wrong in others,
Believing itself pure,
Or hide the truth, forgetting
It always will endure?

Can true love be half-hearted
In what it tries to do?
Christ gave Himself completely:
Should we not love Him too?

How can we then deny Him,
As friend, whose love so true
Has saved us by His passion
From death, so justly due?

Why must our love grow fainter, -
Our caring be so weak?
With strength, assured through Jesus,
For Him we'll surely speak?

His is a love most patient.
In all things He is kind.
With love and deep compassion,
He died for all mankind.

Three things are ours for ever:
When Jesus we confess
And we can be called Christian, -
Faith, hope and love possess!

1Corinthians 13:4-7,13

HARD PEWS

I think I must have counted every hair on the back of the head of the person sitting in the pew in front! Oh, Mr. Jones, you do need a haircut. Really, Mrs. Green, not another perm and I was sure you were going grey, - you were never that auburn! Just look at those shoulders. Keep fit classes can never produce that physique. You must be wearing shoulder-pads in that new jacket! Where did she get that dress? Just look at those seams; she must have made it herself. I couldn't wear anything that colour, and look, the pattern doesn't quite match down the centre. Choose a plain material I always say, - it always looks smart.

I've been blessed with eyes in the back of my head, you know. Mrs. Brown on the row behind doesn't know I can see she is looking just as miserable as ever. I don't think I have ever seen her smile. Mind you, this preacher doesn't help. What is he going on about? He's been ranting on now for at least twenty-five minutes about absolutely nothing in particular and still doesn't seem to have got to the point, but it wouldn't be seen for me not to come. My, I did remember to set the timer for the Sunday roast, didn't I?

Now just imagine if someone were to burst into the church in the middle of the sermon and come running down the aisle waving his arms above his head and shouting 'Alleluia; I've just found Jesus!' Wouldn't that be exciting? I wonder what the reaction would be. Do you think anyone would dare move? Or would there be complete silence?

Surely that someone would expect to find us all praising God. Isn't that, after all, why we're here in God's house?

Revelation 3:14-22

GRACE IS SHARED

In the spirit of our faith we tell
Of Jesus who was raised to life to
Bring us to His presence when we too
Are raised to glory. As the boundless
Grace of God is shared by more and more
We raise our chorus of thanksgiving
To the Father. Praise His Holy Name!

God is Good. Know His grace.
He listens to our prayer and saves us.
Praise His Holy Name!

In the spirit of our faith we tell
Of Jesus who was raised to life to
Bring us to His presence when we too
Are raised to glory. As the boundless
Grace of God is shared by more and more
We raise our chorus of thanksgiving
To the Father. Praise His Holy Name!

God is Love. Know His grace.
He breaks the cords of death that bind us.
Praise His Holy Name!

In the spirit of our faith we tell
Of Jesus who was raised to life to
Bring us to His presence when we too
Are raised to glory. As the boundless
Grace of God is shared by more and more
We raise our chorus of thanksgiving
To the Father. Praise His Holy Name!

God is Life. Know His grace.
He brought us low, but now He saves us.
Praise His Holy Name!

In the spirit of our faith we tell
Of Jesus who was raised to life to
Bring us to His presence when we too
Are raised to glory. As the boundless
Grace of God is shared by more and more
We raise our chorus of thanksgiving
To the Father. Praise His Holy Name!

Psalm 116:1-9,17-19 2Corinthians 4:13-15

FISH, AND BRICKS!

It was one of those dark, wet, winter days. I scurried from doorway to doorway through the city trying to avoid the worst of a downpour and paused for a minute or two beneath overhanging eaves. Opposite was the cathedral, rising dark and gloomy in the middle of the graveyard. Could the building itself be a huge tomb I thought, as I peered at the tower rising in the dimness like a huge headstone; a memorial to Christ? I hurried over the road to the old, oak door of the cathedral, lifted the heavy latch, pushed the door ajar and went inside. I found no dead body there; instead the lighting provided a welcoming glow over a hive of activity. People were quietly busying themselves in their individual ways of acknowledging a risen Christ, whilst others were working to maintain the fabric of the building to enable it to continue to stand as a witness within the community.

Yet Jesus called to the fishermen, 'Come, I'll make you fishers of men!' Would he not have been just a little upset if as a result of his offer they had then pushed their boats out on to the Sea of Galilee, cast their nets and expected to haul in the odd drowning swimmer? Perhaps he did say to Peter, 'Build my church,' but did he then expect Peter to go off and buy bricks? Of course it is convenient to have a place where we can congregate to worship God, but to what extent would Jesus really appreciate how literally we have taken his words? What would he think of the huge buildings we have erected, the way we seem to worship the fabric, and the time and the money spent maintaining them? Do we need the fishing tackle to follow him? Do we need the bricks?

It is perhaps a natural human desire to need to erect a memorial to the one we love. Christians are no exception and over the centuries have erected the world's most spectacular churches and cathedrals, their love of Christ and the Father being so great. But...

Matthew 4:18-22; 16:16-19 Mark 1:16-20

THE CHURCH

Church buildings are a monument
To Christ, who died for us all.
Tall spires point to God's firmament:
Mighty cathedrals enthral!
      In such a hallowed place
      We meet, to seek His face:
      We, who to Christ belong,
      Worship Him there in song.
Our Christ is still the cornerstone!

We are a church, not made with hands, -
Our love in Christ, the building;
A church unbounded, in all lands
Its mission, true, pursuing.
      Until its task is done,
      In faith, we travel on,
      'Till Sin is overthrown,
      God claims the victor's throne,
And Christ returns to claim His own.

John 4:20-24 1Corinthians 3:9-17 2Corinthians 5:1
1Peter 2:4-9 Revelation 21:22

IN SPIRIT AND IN TRUTH

Perhaps like me, over the years, you've heard comments along the following lines. 'I've attended this church all my life, and my parents before me. In fact, my grandparents went to the opening service! If it closes, then that's it – I don't think I'll go anywhere else.' 'Well what's the point of three or four churches here when one would be quite sufficient? There's only about a dozen or so members at any one of them, so think of all that heating and lighting. How can you expect youngsters to come and sit in this sort of atmosphere for an hour?' 'Personally, I like the stained-glass windows at our church and we've got a lovely organ. I simply couldn't worship if it didn't look just like a proper church.'

When David proposed building a house for God to live in, God enquired whether He, Himself, had ever asked previously if He needed a permanent house. The Tabernacle, a temporary transportable construction, had supplied a passing need for His people.

'Believe me,' said Jesus. 'God is a Spirit. True worshippers will not worship here one day. They will worship in spirit and in truth.'

Exodus 40:16-38 2Samuel 7:1-7 John 4:23

56

THE GARDEN OF THE LORD

Gladness and joy will be found in the garden of the Lord
    In the New, Holy, City of our God.
Crowned with everlasting joy, we shall enter the city,
    In the New Heaven and Earth of our God.
We shall worship with thanksgiving and with everlasting song,
And joyfully shout, "Our God is King," for evermore
    Before the throne of God and of the Lamb.

Crystal and clear is the river, which will flow from the throne,
    Through the New Eden planted by our God,
Flanked by trees with healing power, - leaves of peace for the nations, -
    In the New Heaven and Earth of our God.
We shall enter into Zion crowned with everlasting joy
And gratefully eat the fruits of life for evermore
    Before the throne of God and of the Lamb.

God and His son are the only temple there to be found
    In the bright, shining City of our God.
Blessed through ever-dawning day, we shall rest in Their Presence
    In the New Heaven and Earth of our God.
We shall live then as His children and with radiance in our eyes,
And heaven's new song sing and worship bring for evermore
    Before the throne of God and of the Lamb.

Psalm 23:2,6 Isaiah 51:3,11 John 4:21,23
Revelation 21:1-4,22-23; 22:1-5

THE COMPELLING DELUSION

I saw what happened. I witnessed it with my own eyes. I know exactly who is to blame. I am so certain of my facts, I would be prepared to swear even that black is white!

We've never had it so good. Things are getting better all the time. Don't think of changing ships now: how could you possibly trust anyone else. I say, better the devil you know!

Now Paul writes about the coming of the Lord Jesus Christ. 'Don't suddenly lose your heads. You realised that the devil you knew was indeed the devil. You opted for a change but his changing tactics, his differing guises and his tempting promises have not deceived you. Stand firm and hold to the traditions you have learned and God will strengthen you.'

But the wicked, by a compelling delusion, believe what is false, swear that black is white, and prefer the devil they know. They will be excluded from the splendour when the evil one is annihilated by the radiance of Christ's presence.

2Thessalonians 2:1-12

THE SPLENDOUR OF YOUR MIGHT

In the splendour of Your might
Come, Jesus: come.
Come: reveal Your glory to Your own.
Lord, we long for that great day
When our calling is fulfilled.
Come in majesty to bring us to Your throne.

Bless us with Your peace.
May our faith increase
And our love for each grow greater day by day.
Every act inspire
With the Spirit's power,
That we might reflect Your radiance.
Come, we pray.

In the splendour of Your might
Come, Jesus: come.
Come: reveal Your glory to Your own.
Lord, we long for that great day
When our calling is fulfilled.
Come in majesty to bring us to Your throne.

Flame our hearts with fire,
That we never tire
But prove worthy of Your kingdom's glorious call.
Steadfast to remain:
Fellowship sustain, -
For by love we serve, support, and nourish all.

In the splendour of Your might
Come, Jesus: come.
Come: reveal Your glory to Your own.
Lord, we long for that great day
When our calling is fulfilled.
Come in majesty to bring us to Your throne.

Come Lord. Claim Your own,
As in love we've grown.
Glorify Your Name among us with Your grace.
Saviour, we adore,
Love and praise the more,
Longing for the joyous time we see Your face.

In the splendour of Your might
Come, Jesus: come.
Come: reveal Your glory to Your own.
Lord, we long for that great day
When our calling is fulfilled.
Come in majesty to bring us to Your throne.

2 Thessalonians 1

59

THE BIG SPEND

It seems that whenever the slightest incident occurs crowds begin to gather. Just one or two people may stop and stare at first, but in no time at all a huge crowd has gathered. Ask someone on the fringe what has happened and usually they haven't a clue. Crowds seemed to follow Jesus everywhere he went. Some joined him to listen and learn, but others just to gawk or grumble.

Are we really just following the crowd at Christmas? Do we allow ourselves to get caught up in high-pressure exploitation or do we really want to listen and learn from the retelling of the Christmas story as we remember the birth of the Christ Child and offer our gifts? Do we forget that the baby born in humble surroundings grew up to befriend sinners and strangers? We have prospered through the strength he gives and the blessings we have received or are we conceited enough to believe that all we have is for us alone and achieved only by our own efforts?

As Christmas approaches each year, may the Giver of Life call us into new harmonies of care. So may we never neglect to share what we have with others, particularly remembering those less fortunate than ourselves. Like the apostle Paul, may we see how God's gift of grace to us was designed for the benefit of others, and may the mind that was in Christ Jesus be implanted in us, casting out self-will and self-seeking.

Isaiah 55:2 Matthew 25:37-45 Ephesians 3:1-2

60

THE GREATEST GIFT

A babe was born in Bethlehem,
Long, long ago.
From highest heaven God sent a King,
Through lowly birth, His love to bring
And peace to know.

The greatest gift at Christmas time
God gave us all.
The King of Kings, in swaddling clothes,
A stable for His palace chose, -
A humble stall.

Each Christmas now, our gifts we send
At great expense,
But if we give with selfish thought,
In spirit not as God first taught,
Can this make sense?

Does Christmas summon our goodwill
To help the poor, -
Or are we dazed by needless greed,
And feast, and scoff at others' need?
God, make us sure.

We celebrate Christ's birth with joy
And mirth each year,
Yet still could help the old awhile,
Or try to make some poor child smile
With Christmas cheer.

When stars in heaven at Christmas shine
On crisp, white, snow,
Or fairy lights on tinselled tree
In glitt'ring windows dance, may we
God's true gift, know?

Luke 2:10-11 John 3:16 Romans 5:15; 6:23

THE CAVE OF THE NATIVITY

Any visit to the Holy Land would be incomplete without a visit to Bethlehem, walking across Manger Square, stooping low to enter the Church of the Nativity and gazing down on the spot where the birth of Jesus almost certainly took place. My first visit, therefore, was incomplete, not that I didn't go to Bethlehem, or bow my head to pass through the low doorway, or even descend to the Grotto of the Nativity. I simply missed seeing the fourteen-pointed silver star on the white marble floor bearing the words that translated from the Latin reads 'Here Jesus Christ was born to the Virgin Mary.' It wasn't that I didn't look for the star, it was simply because the cave was so crammed with people all jostling to see the manger or the spot marking the birth, it proved impossible to see what they were all looking at before I had to leave. Such was my disappointment, that I resolved I would return to Bethlehem one day but this time ensure that I did see the star. And so I did, some years later, and I was overjoyed to find that only a small group was permitted to enter the Grotto at any one time and I had a magnificent unimpeded view of the entire manger and silver star.

Mary and Joseph with the new-born child had occupied the stable alone whilst the town was crowded with people unaware of the birth of the Son of God. At the end of the second millennia the town lay virtually empty, besieged perhaps by descendants of people who had been forced to flock to the town by reason of the census ordered by the Emperor Augustus. Ironically, many thousands of intending worshippers were denied the opportunity of attending the Church of the Nativity to mark the two thousandth anniversary of Christ's birth and seeing the place where he was born.

Luke 2:15

HAVE YOU BEEN?

Have you been to Bethlehem:
Have you seen the shining star?
Have you been like three wise men:
Have you journeyed from afar?
　　Have you been: have you been: have you been?
　　Come now!

Have you been to Bethlehem
On the hills where flocks still graze?
Have you watched like shepherds watched:
Have you joined the angels' praise?
　　Have you been: have you been: have you been?
　　Come now!

Have you been to Bethlehem:
Have you seen the manger there?
Have you seen the Holy Child:
Have you offered Him a prayer?
　　Have you been: have you been: have you been?
　　Come now!

Have you been to Bethlehem,
To the birthplace of a King
Born to reign for evermore
And eternal peace to bring?
　　Holy Child, Son of God, King of Love, -
　　I come!

Matthew 2:1-2 Luke 1:31-33; 2:6-16

CAN THINGS BE DIFFERENT?

I believe in angels! That may sound crazy, but the Bible contains ample evidence for their existence. I'm no biblical scholar, but apart from the mention of God - the Father, Son and Holy Spirit - and God's chosen people, angels probably feature more often than does any other subject in the Bible. Indeed, angels are consistent in appearing right through the Bible from Genesis to the Revelation of John.

In Acts, reference is made to Peter's angel and in the closing verses of the New Testament Jesus mentions his own angel. Earlier, during Christ's ministry, he takes a little child and then says that to enter the Kingdom of Heaven one must become like little children, and refers to their angels in heaven.

Just as the two followers of Jesus failed to recognise him on the Emmaus Road, there are times when perhaps we have walked with an angel but failed to realise its presence, possibly because we have been preoccupied with our own affairs or self-importance.

Although I know of no basis for saying so, it may be that we each have two angels. Not all angels are apparently flying at God's command and it may be that we each have a good angel and an evil angel who tussle with each other as well as vying to lead us in one direction or another. Could we change the course of events or be a different person if we really took the time to listen to the angels?

Matthew 18:1-3,10 Acts 12:7-15 Hebrews 1:13-14
Revelation 22:16

LISTEN TO THE ANGELS

If I'd been close to Bethlehem
With shepherds and their sheep,
All huddled on a mountainside,
Afraid to fall asleep,
Would I have thought it was a dream
When angels filled the sky
Announcing that the Son of God
Had just been born nearby?

Listen to the angels.
Hear what they say.
Go and find the Christ Child,
Born for you this day.

If I had gone and peeped with them
Around the stable door,
Would I have known "Emmanuel"
Was lying in the straw?
Dare I have told His mother that
I'd heard an angel sing,
"Go now, and find a new-born Child,
And worship Him as King?"

Listen to the angels.
Hear what they say.
Go and find the Christ Child,
Born for you this day.

If I'd have been amongst the crowd
That thronged the inn that night,
And tried to tell them I had seen
A wondrous, heavenly sight,
Would they have listened to me as
I struggled hard to say
The answer to their hopes and fears
Was snuggled in the hay?

Listen to the angels.
Hear what they say.
Go and find the Christ Child,
Born for you this day.

And will the people listen now
Two thousand years have run,
Or find no room within their hearts,
Rejecting God's own Son?
Then seek the new-born Child today
And heed the angels' song, -
"Let peace and joy reign in your
hearts"
And right the years of wrong.

Listen to the angels.
Hear what they say.
Go and find the Christ Child,
Born for you this day.

Isaiah 7:14 Matthew 1:23 Luke 2:7-14

GETTING INTO CREDIT

It had been one of those beautiful starry nights. Whilst gazing up into the heavens I realised just how little I knew about what even a single star is and I resolved as a starting point to see firstly how the dictionary defined a star. My eyes soon wandered over the page and fixed upon the word *starr*, a word I had not known before. I discovered that a starr is a Jewish deed or bond, one that clears a person's debt or releases him from it.

A new star is said to herald the birth of a king. The star denotes where the king has been born or could there be more to it than meets the eye?

In two opposing schools of thought, the one person may say 'I've seen it all before so you can't tell me any differently. The outcome is quite obvious so it's not worth another glance.' The other person in fact may say 'I believe there's more to it than meets the eye.'

The apostle Paul refers to things beyond our seeing and hearing, God's secret purpose from the very beginning, which an unspiritual person cannot grasp because he is only able to judge things by the world's standard. The gospel is that secret purpose, how God in His wisdom brings us to our destined glory.

Do we only see a star announcing the birth of Jesus or do we see the secret purpose hidden by its brightness? Can we see through the brightness the hand of God moving to release us from our debt?

Matthew 2:1-2,7-10; 18:23-35 1Corinthians 2:7-15

THE BETHLEHEM STAR

On Christmas Day, God spoke to me,
"Tis I, the First and Last. Fear not!"
I hid my eyes lest I should see
The splendour of His Majesty
And die on that dread spot.

"Be not afraid." I heard Him say.
"Look up, and gaze into the sky.
The star you see, in bright array,
Shines for My Son, who's born today.
Think not that you must die."

I raised my head and fixed my sight
On that great star. Yes, it was true.
A dazzling shaft of shining light
Shot earthwards, shattering shades of night.
I trembled at the view.

A cross of white, the star appeared,
That stretched from earth to heaven above.
Then suddenly my vision cleared,
And hanging on the cross, appeared
A Man, whose face was love.

As if I'd stared straight at the sun
And blind become with spots, like blood,
A stream of crimson seemed to run
Down from His side, the side of one
So meek, yet pure, and good.

"Son of My Son, - you have today
Experienced love, - a Father's care, -
Through birth, then death, rebirth, I say
Is truly yours this Christmas Day,
And endless love we share!"

I knelt and prayed. "My God, forgive
A child so blind with foolish pride,
That I might ever for Christ live,
Example take, love freely give
For love of Him who died."

Luke 2:9-11 Acts 2:17-24, 32-36

ORANGES AND LEMONS

'Oranges and lemons' say the bells of St. Clement's. 'When will you pay me' say the bells of Old Bailey? May we cross your Chinese waters in our silver boat? Yes – if you're wearing green! Matthew, Mark, Luke and John! Childhood chants, street games! What were they all about? What did some of the words really mean?

An inquisitive child was asking his mother questions. 'Well son, Matthew, Mark, Luke and John, they're the first four books of the New Testament, aren't they? The gospels, you know! And they were four of the twelve disciples.' The gospels, New Testament, Old Testament! But what are they? 'Well my boy, they're obviously old and new books. You've heard them say in church, today's reading from the scriptures is from the epistle or the gospel.' Yes mum, but what is it – the gospel? Why don't they say? 'Well listen son, they preach the gospel.' Preach it! What is preaching? 'Well it's the sermon. It's part of the church service.' But they seem to read the sermon and read the gospel. What's the difference? 'Well the gospel – it's good news.' Not like in the newspapers or on television then? That always seems to be bad news dad says. 'No, it's the good news of Jesus.' Yes, but I still don't know what the gospel is? What is the good news? Why doesn't anyone answer my question? Why does everyone talk about the gospel and good news without saying what it really is?

Romans 1:16; 3:21-26

WHAT IS THIS GOOD NEWS?

What is this good news of Jesus
Who lived in Galilee by a lake; -
Who walked on water; - calmed the stormy
Rushing waves for His friends' sake?

Why did He give those with blindness sight; -
And bring the dead to life; -
And feed the crowds while He talked of peace?
Yet all He caused was strife!

What was the point of going
To where He knew His life would end, -
Even as He prayed, betrayed
By one He had chosen for a friend?

The mystery has been revealed, -
Why on a cross He died -
But was raised to life, and now lives for ever,
Reigning by His Father's side.

Our wicked ways had driven us
Far from our Maker's side.
But to bring us back and make right our wrongs, -
That is why God's Son, Jesus, died.

Matthew 8:23-27; 14:22-33; 15:29-38; 26:1-2,36,47-48
Galatians 1:1-12 Ephesians 1:3-10

THE PROJECT

Poor Roger! Just look at him chewing his biro. He's absolutely lost to the world. He'll never get to the youth club tonight. He must still be working on the class homework project. He must be taking it really seriously. I finished mine moons ago. Ask him what topic he was given.

Oops, Roge! Trust you to draw the short straw! It must have been a joke question. 'Is Jesus Christ living near you? Provide proof in your answer.' Our subjects were so easy. Only took twenty minutes altogether! Why waste time over it Roger when it's clearly a hoax. Just write 'no.' Surely you know Jesus Christ died two millennia ago.

Well, his friends seem to have gone off without him. I'll tell him I couldn't help overhearing the conversation, as it was rather high-spirited. Take no notice of their ridicule, Roger. Have a good wander round the village and jot down all that you see. Then make your own mind up. You may get quite a surprise before you've finished your project!

Romans 12:2 1Thessalonians 5:21

OPEN YOUR EYES

How would you like to find Jesus?
Open your eyes; look around you.
Walk round the village and note what you see,
But don't be surprised!
You'll find fishermen down by the river,
And sheep up on the hillside;
There're donkeys, horses, and ponies to ride.
You'll see more besides, if you
Open your eyes!

Yet surprise; will you find Jesus?
Use your eyes; can He be hidden away?
Has He walked with you, or passed by you:
Is He behind locked doors? Are you sure?

Down Main Street you may find dancing,
Drama, playgroups, or scouting.
Walk round the village and note what you see,
But don't be surprised!
Sponsored walks are held by the river:
A man stands by the roadside,
Selling his flags for the homeless or poor.
There's much more besides, if you
Open your eyes!

Yet surprise; will you find Jesus?
Use your eyes; can He be hidden away?
Has He walked with you, or passed by you:
Is He behind locked doors? Are you sure?

Can you hear the laughter of children,
Or feel the warmth of the sunshine,
And see all the smiles of the friends you know,
And gleam in their eyes?
Hear the church bells ring near the river;
The beck gush down the hillside;
But hush, by the churchyard, where saints rest who've died,
'Though one day will rise to meet
Christ in the skies!

Yet surprise; will you find Jesus?
Use your eyes; can He be hidden away?
Has He walked with you, or passed by you:
Is He behind locked doors? Are you sure?

Luke 24:13-16

71

THE SUGGESTION

If I'm to start looking for Jesus, where do you suggest I start? There are so many places he might be and such a lot of ground to cover. I haven't a great deal of time and with such a lot going on around here, where would be the best place to begin?

Well, you'll find the church is right in the centre of the village. You can't miss it, can you? It has a very fine spire and there's a clock, so you'll be able to keep an eye on the time. Outside the church, you'll find a notice board showing the name of the church and maybe a name and address or two. It may also tell you the times of the services but don't worry, I think you'll find the door is unlocked during the daytime so it may be a good idea to start by looking inside.

Matthew 7:7-8 Luke 11:9-10

INSIDE THE CHURCH

Where can Jesus be?
Is He hidden from me?
Inside the church it's cold and bare, -
No sign of Him anywhere!
Where can Jesus be?

Tell me, is it true:
Is He known to you?
Inside the church it's cold and bare, -
Surely Jesus can't be there!
Tell me: is it true?

Why this Jesus fuss?
Hardly lives with us!
Inside the church it's cold and bare, -
Would He visit people there?
Why this Jesus fuss?

Where can Jesus be?
It's not clear to me!
Inside the church it's cold and bare, -
P'rhaps I'd better look elsewhere!
Where can Jesus be?

Where could Jesus hide?
By the riverside?
Up on the hill? There's no one there, -
Or the Square, as I'm aware!
Where could Jesus hide?

Matthew 24:10-12 Luke 12:35-37

THE SHORT STRAW

What a title for a homework project! 'Prove whether or not Jesus Christ lives anywhere near you.' How can you be expected to write a whole essay on a subject like that! Why was everyone else given such easy topics to write about? Just my luck! It must be a joke. Then why am I taking the whole thing so seriously? I must be crazy. Why didn't I take the others' advice and simply answer 'no.' I would be with them all at the youth club by now having a great time. When I opened the church door and peered inside I really did believe it would be easy to find out all I needed to know to answer the question posed. Now what do I do? Where do I go from here?

Come on, Roger, we're all waiting for you. Leave all that nonsense alone. You've been conned, man! Don't be so wet. Don't be crazy!

1Corinthians 1:25-27

DON'T BE CRAZY

Don't be crazy. What a lot of nonsense.
Don't be crazy. What a lot of nonsense!
Don't be crazy! What a lot of nonsense!

How can you be sure that Jesus,
Jesus is still with us here today?
Don't be stupid: look around you:
People dress in jeans and watch T.V.
And we drive our motor cars:
To shop at supermarkets, call:
No more miracles and wonders, -
There's N.H.S. for all!

We all now own videos:
We don't need to go to shows:
We store all we need to know on disc.
They said you reap what you sow:
To heaven or hell you go:
What nonsense! We've all we could wish.

It's silly, - so silly. You be silly, - be so!
What a lot of nonsense! What a bore!
Quick, hurry, - you scurry: hurry if you must go
Looking for a man who lives no more.
Look round the church, - in the car park, - by the river,
Any corner He could hide:
Come and tell us when you've found Him,
And then you'll know He died!
Go and search around the village.
You'll prove that He has died.

Psalm 83:1-3 2Peter 2:1-3,17-21

WALKING AROUND BLINDFOLDED

I'm absolutely shattered! I've walked around every inch of this village. I've had a good look at everything. I happened to bump into a friend of mine who was shopping for her grandmother who is housebound at present. While we stood chatting, there was an old man trying to cross the road so we had to break off to assist him. He had a white stick. On the other side of the road I noticed the lady who lives next door to me. She was coming out of the Post Office where she had been to fetch old Mr. Green's pension for him. He suffered a stroke and hasn't been able to get out since. I suddenly thought I might find some useful information for my essay in the library. I couldn't help but think how cluttered the notice board is getting just as you go in. There're posters about Age Concern, Red Cross, Shelter, Save the Children, Guide Dogs, Mencap, Cancer Concern, Alzheimer's – I could go on! If I were to be involved with just a couple of those concerns when I've left school I don't think I'd have the time to go to work! The things people do. It's amazing. It makes you wonder why they want to get involved when there're so many other exciting things to do. Then who should I find inside the library but my ex-girlfriend, Miss do-goody. This time she was changing extra-large print books for someone who her parents give a lift to church on Sundays.

I don't believe it! The penny's just dropped! Have I really been walking around blindfolded all this time? Have I only just opened my eyes?

Isaiah 35:5-6 Matthew 5:16 1Peter 2:12

I FOUND HIM

I searched and found that Jesus lives
Here with us, now, today.
And as I found Him by my side,
I'll let Him show the way.
I found Him by the riverside:
My friends showed me His care:
In fact, the more I looked for Him,
I found Him everywhere!

As children laughed, I heard His voice:
I saw Him as folk smiled.
Yet I found some who owned Him not,
And His pure name defiled.
But He is here, for all to find.
He can our lives renew.
My happiness is quite complete, -
O may you find Him too.

John 1:40-41,45

TWO THOUSAND YEARS OF AGE!

How blind can you be! How dumb! He is here; Jesus is alive! To think I've been going around expecting to find some guy who looks two thousand years old! Of course you don't see the colour of the sky if you skip along trying to avoid all the cracks in the pavement, do you? It all fits in, doesn't it, what they used to say in Sunday School, before I stopped going there? I remember the story now of that fellow on his way to Jericho who was attacked by thieves. Someone came along and took pity on him after others had walked by without stopping to see what was wrong. I reckon they called his helper the Good Samaritan. Then there was a young kid who shared his bread and fish with thousands of people. I bet he got into trouble when he arrived home because I think he was shopping for his mother! And didn't they say we have to love our enemies? That's tough! I seem to remember there were even people who made a hole in a roof to lower a sick man down so he could see Jesus. He was so desperate and it was impossible to get near the door because of the crowds.

I didn't think things like this happened in this day and age, but I'm not so sure now. What about that party in the old people's home last Christmas? Everyone was so generous. And the blind people taken to the late-night shopping when there's not so much of a crush? I know some friends who are taking handicapped children to the seaside next week. They always put on a surprise meal or give them a special treat before coming home.

I think Jesus must be – sort of invisible! .

Matthew 5:44 Mark 2:1-5 Luke 6:27,35; 10:30-37
John 6:1-13

YOU ARE HERE!

Invisible Jesus, we know You are here.
As we look around us, Your presence is clear.
Your Spirit You've sent as Your strength by our side.
Your truth is in all things: Your beauty, our guide.

We've seen You in ways that our eyes could not show.
Your voice, though familiar, we just did not know.
Your Spirit beside us, we failed to entreat:
Though awed by Your presence, - yet still did not meet!

But now that our ears are attuned to Your voice,
And eyes have been opened, our hearts now rejoice.
May we show the doubters where You may be found
So all may, believing, in Your joy abound?

Invisible Jesus, we know You are here.
As we look around us, Your presence is clear.
Your Spirit You've sent as Your strength by our side.
Your truth is in all things: Your beauty, our guide.

Acts 1:1-3 Colossians 1:15 1Timothy 1:15-17 1Peter 1:8

CRIPPLED FROM BIRTH

The view from the office window was quite beautiful, overlooking the gateway to the proud city. One could gaze down on a roundabout, which was always planted immaculately in a blaze of colour, no matter what the season. Lime trees and blossom trees lined the carriageway and ornate lampposts were adorned with hanging baskets filled with flowers in trailing profusion. The scene painted a picture of affluence and attractiveness for both visitor and resident alike.

Each day, a vagrant came and sat on the cold, hard pavement on the street corner, his back resting against the railings that separated pedestrians from the busy traffic. His clothing was the same whatever the weather, hanging in tatters about him. His hands and face were dirty, and thin long wisps of hair blew about his head. He was a picture of absolute wretchedness and deprivation. The busy world around him went about its business from hour to hour and day to day!

A cripple from birth lay begging by the temple gate that was called Beautiful. Peter and John, as they approached, looked down on him with compassion. Seeing their concern for him, the cripple put out his hand. 'Sorry mate,' said Peter, 'but we're just about skint ourselves, though what we do have is Jesus within our hearts. He's the great teacher and healer, and we can share with you his many rich blessings.'

Acts 3:1-16

THE DAWN OF HEALING

God, whose grace upon the world
Dawned with healing for mankind,
Grants us hope of heavenly splendour,
Leaving worldly ways behind.

God, Redeemer of the world,
Saves with His life-giving power;
Gift, by sacrificial favour,
Of the Saviour's dying hour.

God, the Spirit in the world,
Purifies, makes all things new.
Holy Spirit heal, renew us,
Cleanse, reclaim our hearts for you.

Trinity of love and power,
Heal and set our hearts aflame.
Holy Spirit, burn within us
With the love of Jesu's name.

Titus 2:11-15; 3:3-8

GONE FOR A SONG

Please, please don't ask me to help out. I'm very rusty: I haven't sung properly in years.

Mind you, I did sing in the choir at school. We won a prize at the music festival whilst I was with the school choir. We knew how to sing properly in those days. I had such a beautiful voice and the teacher said I had perfect pitch. Not many people have, you know! She always insisted that I stood right in the middle of the front row. I know I was always pretty - the other girls were just jealous – but it was nothing to do with my looks really. I can't stand older women who still think they can sing soprano as if they were still in their teens. I say you shouldn't attempt to sing after you're forty – forty-five at the most. Mind you, I do like to watch Songs of Praise, as long as it's none of that new-fangled rubbish. Give me the good old ones that we all know, that's what I always say.

Never mind. I can still look forward to singing with the heavenly choir one day as long as Peter is standing at the gate of heaven handing out some miracle throat spray or whatever. You'll just have to count me out for now but I'm sure someone else will be willing to help.

Luke 14:18-20

SING PRAISE TO GOD

Sing out in praise, our hearts, to God.
Join with the myriad angels' choir.
Acclaim His majesty and power.
Sing out in praise, our hearts, to God.
Our sweetest melody aspire
To sing, in praise, to God.

For we have come, perfected by the sprinkled blood.
For we have come, enrolled in heaven our name.
For we have come, as God fore-planned we should.
'Tis heaven to sing Your praise, our hearts and lips proclaim.

Sing out in praise, our hearts, to God.
Join with the myriad angels' choir.
Acclaim His majesty and power.
Sing out in praise, our hearts, to God.
Our sweetest melody aspire
To sing, in praise, to God.

For we believe that Jesus is the Father's Son.
For we believe He died to set us free.
For we believe the victory He's won.
'Tis heaven to know one day we face to face shall be.

Sing out in praise, our hearts, to God.
Join with the myriad angels' choir.
Acclaim His majesty and power.
Sing out in praise, our hearts, to God.
Our sweetest melody aspire
To sing, in praise, to God.

For we adore You, Father God. We sing Your praise.
For we adore You, Jesus Christ our Lord.
For we adore You, - set our hearts ablaze.
'Tis heaven to sing "for ever be Your Name adored."

Sing out in praise, our hearts, to God.
Join with the myriad angels' choir.
Acclaim His majesty and power.
Sing out in praise, our hearts, to God.
Our sweetest melody aspire
To sing, in praise, to God.

Psalm 81:1-2 Hebrews 12:22-24, 28-29

THE CORONATION

I remember clearly the Coronation of Her Majesty Queen Elizabeth. My parents didn't have a television set at that time, but the whole family, together with uncles, aunts and cousins, were invited to my grandparents' home to watch the ceremony and celebrations in London and indeed the entire kingdom as events unfolded on their television. We all sat in awe as we watched the pageantry for hour after hour, hardly daring to leave the room for refreshments spread out on the dining room table in case we should miss some critical moment. Never before had so many subjects been able to witness the coronation of their monarch live as the events took place.

We were schoolchildren at the time and the County Education Authority decided it would be fitting to make a presentation to every pupil to mark the occasion. A ceremony was held at which each child was given a specially bound edition of the New Testament. On the front of the black hard-back cover was embossed in gold lettering 'To Commemorate the Coronation of Her Majesty Queen Elizabeth 2 June 1953.'

Inside the book was a preface containing a message from the Director and Chairman of the Education Committee. It stated that the Bible and the New Testament remained the most precious possession of the British Nation, and indeed the whole world. It referred to Her Majesty's first Christmas broadcast on 25 December 1952 when she reminded us all how much the future of this country depended upon the ways in which we practise the virtues of the Christian family in the world at large. It explained to us that The Queen would be presented with a Bible when she was crowned in Westminster Abbey and that the Archbishop of Canterbury would pronounce that the Book was the most valuable thing that this world affords.

Cont'd on page 86

THIS ROYAL THRONE OF KINGS
A sonnet for a Jubilee

What I, an unknown sonneteer, compose
Some mighty work to celebrate a year
Of sovereign's jubilation! Yea, I fear
My hand, unskilled for lines of royal prose,
Might well wild brier portray our native rose,
Or knights with want of shining arms, appear
With tarnished coat of mail and fail to steer
A kingdom's fall to victory o'er her foes.
Shall trumpeters their silver trumpets sound
In flawless fanfare for the monarch's reign
And blaze from bonfires on far hills be found
To kindle kingdom's hope, and trust regain?
Then, shall our song of Jubilee resound,
"Eternal, may this throne of kings remain!"

Psalm 45:1-6 Ecclesiastes 9:10-11

The Moderator of the General Assembly of the Church of Scotland would add 'Here is Wisdom; This is the royal Law; These are the lively Oracles of God.' In presenting us with our own copy of the New Testament, we were asked to look to it as a symbol of the best things in our British way of life, trusting that it would inspire and guide us through our lives. At her coronation, The Queen made her vows and she would be helped to keep these vows with the prayers and help of her people.

I still have my copy of the New Testament to this very day, although I found it hidden away in a dark corner with other old papers. I am ashamed to admit that I never read the actual copy. Perhaps I did not wish to spoil its mint condition - or could that just be an excuse? But Her Majesty Queen Elizabeth has faithfully kept the vows she made that day and I'm glad she was crowned 'Defender of the Faith.' I wonder if now we would have the courage and wisdom to make a similar symbolic gift to the present generation of schoolchildren and whether we still firmly believe that our laws and way of life should have biblical foundation?

Hallelujah, for the Lord God Omnipotent reigns and the kingdom of this world has become the kingdom of our Lord and His Christ whose reign shall never end!

Ecclesiastes 5: 1-7
1 Peter 1:5-7

THE
JOHN BETJEMAN
AWARD

Presented in memory of Sir John Betjeman
by The Society for the Protection of Ancient Buildings
for exemplary repairs to churches and
chapels in England and Wales
remaining in use.

TENTERDEN METHODIST
CHURCH. KENT
for the repair of the war memorial pipe organ

Inglesham Church, Wiltshire, by John Piper. The Church was repaired according to
the principles of The Society for the Protection of Ancient Buildings, through the energy
and help of William Morris, its founder. It was a favourite of John Betjeman.

The John Betjeman Award Certificate mentioned on the back cover

87

TIME TO REFLECT

There is nothing new in the idea of Christians meeting together in their homes in addition to attending church for services of divine worship and communion. In the letter to the Hebrews, we are urged not to stay away but to meet for the purpose of deepening our love and understanding of each other and to encourage one another to go on to reach our full potential for good works in Christ's name.

Such is the way our church meets, calling the house group 'Time to Reflect.' There is no immovable venue, no fixed format for the meeting, no compulsion to take an active role and no guarantee there will always be the same people together, but it would be unusual if certain key elements were not present. We may include something as simple as a story written especially for children or reflect on a deeper meditation or religious commentary. Some time may be spent listening to music or we may reflect for a while individually in silence. We may read poetry, or the words of a hymn, or passages of scripture, but there will always be a time in whatever form it may take when we are clearly taking part in an act of worship. This will involve adoration or praise, a time of thanksgiving, a time of petition or intercession and a time of confession. The meal we usually share may only be just a cup of tea or coffee with biscuits, but from time to time we also share in the body and blood of Christ in a simple act of remembrance.

Christ may be both the Alpha and the Omega, but he is also so much more in between. There can never be a limit to our capacity to ponder and reflect. May we all make 'Time to Reflect!'

Acts 2:42,46-47 Hebrews 10:24-25 Revelation 22:13

PONDER IT IN YOUR HEART

Contemplate the birth of Jesus;
Ponder it within your heart,
As His mother, Mary, marvelled
Lovingly within her heart.
Jesus, Jesus, we adore You,
Worship, worship You as King!
Here, we lay our hearts before You.
Child, accept the gifts we bring.

Listen to the words of Mary
When the guests had drawn the wine.
"Do whatever Jesus tells you."
He will change your hearts and mine.
Jesus, Jesus, we adore You,
Worship, worship You as King!
Here, we lay our hearts before You.
Lord, accept the love we bring.

Ponder 'neath the cross with Mary:
Pause and gaze upon her Son.
See His arms outstretched with mercy:
Hear His shout of victory won.
Jesus, Jesus, we adore You,
Worship, worship You as King!
Here, we lay our hearts before You.
Take, O Lamb, the sins we bring.

Ponder with the saints, like Mary,
How her Son will come again,
Coming in a cloud with glory,
Coming with His angels' train.
Jesus, Jesus, we adore You,
Worship, worship You as King!
Here, we lay our hearts before You.
Judge, accept the lives we bring.

Ponder how in heaven, with Mary
And the saints, before the Throne
We shall bow in awesome wonder,
Called by God to be His own.
Jesus, Jesus, we adore You,
Worship, worship You as King!
Father, Son and Holy Spirit,
Here, accept the praise we bring.

Matthew 2:11; 16:27 Luke 2:19; 21:27
John 1:29; 2:1-5; 19:25-30 1Peter 2:9-10
Revelation 22:3-4

BEYOND TWELFTH NIGHT

Christmas-time is over. The fairy lights and tinsel have given way to short frosty days and long dark nights. The parties have ended, the pantomime had its final curtain and Santa's grotto has been dismantled for another year. Everywhere seems so plain. The holly and the mistletoe have been thrown away and all those cheery cards from relatives and the so many friends we have known over the passing years have all been taken down. There's no more turkey and trimmings, Christmas pudding or crackers. The Christmas tree and its treasured decorations have been carefully packed away. Even by now, a few new toys are laying somewhat dejected in a dark corner.

What then, does the little child now remember of the Christmas story? Did the nativity play even tell the Christmas Story? 'Well, mum, there was Mary and Joseph, and the baby Jesus. They were in a stable with animals. Oh and there were lots of angels singing "Hallelujah." What does hallelujah mean, mum?'

'It means "everyone sing a happy song to God" I think. Fancy, it was a world premiere for the angels song, and yet they performed it to simple shepherds of all people, in an open-air theatre!'

Luke 2:8-14

THE HOLY FAMILY

A carol for Mary,
Most favoured of all,
Who brought forth the Saviour
In Bethlehem's stall.
   Angels singing; Peace He's bringing; Hear bells ringing;
   See the star brightly shining over Bethlehem.
   Bethlehem! Hallelujah! See the star!

A carol for Joseph,
Strong, steadfast, yet mild,
"The Son of God, - Jesus"
He named the dear child.
   Angels singing; Peace He's bringing; Hear bells ringing;
   See the star brightly shining over Bethlehem.
   Bethlehem! Hallelujah! See the star!

A carol for Jesus,
"God with us" on Earth.
Incarnate Redeemer.
Rejoice For His birth!
   Angels singing; Peace He's bringing; Hear bells ringing;
   See the star brightly shining over Bethlehem.
   Bethlehem! Hallelujah! See the star!

A carol with angels:
Sing with Heaven's choir
"All glory to God," for
His gift, - the Messiah!
   Angels singing; Peace He's bringing; Hear bells ringing;
   See the star brightly shining over Bethlehem.
   Bethlehem! Hallelujah! See the star!

Matthew 1:20-25; 2:9-11 Luke 1:28-31; 2:11-14

RAINBOWS

As the eve of Christmas 2000 approached I, like many others, was filled with optimism that at long last we may start to witness a new dawn of love, joy and peace, and that the world may begin to turn away from sorrow, hatred and warfare. Surely the two thousandth anniversary of Christ's birth would mark a new awakening in the hearts and minds of man? I recalled the words of a carol I had written years previously giving an assurance that Mary gave birth to the Hope of the World.

I was filled with dismay seeing the television news reports from Bethlehem. Only a handful of worshippers were likely to dare approach the town on such a momentous occasion. As I witnessed the scenes of destruction in the besieged town, in my mind I rewrote the first verse of that carol, completing a new version to reflect the birthday 2000 as Christmas ended.

But the cameraman, who had filmed from inside a building brought to rubble, had inadvertently captured another image through an open doorway. There was a fleeting glance of a distant rainbow. The God of Creation was reminding us that He is still the God of Redemption brought about by the gift of His Son who would give His life but rise again to fulfil God's plan for mankind. The rainbow was also a reminder that God still restrains His wrath despite man's inhumanity to man.

Genesis 9:12-14 Revelation 4:3

BIRTHDAY 2000

Gone, seems the babe, from the manger of hay.
Where is the Hope of the World, born that day?
Timbers hang splintered, where once was a stall:
Guests have deserted the bomb-blasted hall.

Soldiers wage war on the mountain nearby.
Dark is the town, whilst their flares light the sky.
Distant, the rumble of gunfire 'til dawn
Breaks upon Bethlehem, downcast, forlorn.

Where now the angels the shepherds heard sing?
What have become of those gifts for a king?
Where once for love, joy and peace, there was room,
Sorrow, and hatred, and warfare now loom.

Prophesies, old, still forgotten, still true:
God's love, - His plan for mankind will renew.
Still, the Lamb cries from that manger of hay
'I am the Hope of the World still, this day.'

Matthew 24:4-8

BLAME THE SAWDUST

Early years of academic pressure at school were relieved by happy hours spent in the woodwork room mastering the techniques of mortise and tenon or dovetail joints. Such advanced carpentry only followed the novices achievement in the world of boat building – joining together two planks of wood and adding a funnel, then making it float! The room was swept clean of sawdust to end each lesson. However, my most endearing memory of those days is of the unmistakable aroma, which rose from the glue pot, which permanently bubbled away in one corner of the room over a low flame. This glue had strength to bind any conceivable human error or slip of the chisel.

Noah was the first carpenter to try his hand at boat building. Clouds of sawdust must have formed as he cut planks to size to form his ark. He kept his eyes clear of any specks in order to complete his task but the jeering onlookers were blinded by the dust which seemed like planks in their own eyes. They refused to let Noah rescue them from their wickedness. But Noah relied on the strength of God to seal the door and make the ark watertight.

Despite all his teaching in parables, all the miracles he performed, when Jesus returned to his hometown the people greeted him with 'His mother married a carpenter, and he's only a simple carpenter too! His words are like sawdust blowing from Joseph's workshop! He won't change the way we see things.' But earlier, Jesus had spent forty days and nights in the wilderness where he cleared his own eyes. He saw his task was to build the ark of the new covenant that he would seal with the power of his own life's blood.

Can we see then what Jesus wants us to do for him now,
some two thousand years later, or shall we still just blame the sawdust?

Genesis 6:5 – 9:17 Luke 4:1-30; 6:41-42

LIVING – FOR CHRIST

Christ's hands are our hands –
To do His work, each day.
Christ's feet are our feet –
To lead along His way.
Christ's lips are our lips –
His kindly words to say.
Christ's help is our help –
To bring back who may stray.

We are God's message
In every present age;
Our lives His Bible –
Each life a different page.

(based on words found in a church in Rennes)

Galatians 2:20

95

WATER FILTERS

I live in a region with notoriously hard water and it is always a pleasure when visiting soft water areas, to experience the extra lather when washing one's hands and feel how softer the skin is afterwards. It is not surprising, therefore, to find a water softener in my house and a water filter next to my kettle. The cartridges need frequent replacement to ensure that impurities and unpleasant tastes are filtered effectively away.

Water in biblical times was often hard to come by and could well be infected and so wine or milk was a common drink. A river was a permanent all the year round watercourse even if it was like a mere trickle to us. Otherwise, it was a wadi if it only flowed in the rainy season.

Northeast of Nazareth lies the small village of Kafr Kana, which at the time of Christ was called Cana. It is set in a valley where cacti and pomegranate trees grow and the two churches there mark the site of the first miracle performed by Jesus at the wedding feast. Perhaps it was the impure water that effectively flowed through him to become the choicest wine for those who would drink? Unlike the cartridge in my water filter, his love and purity are changeless.

John 2:7-8

HEAVEN'S LOVE

Heaven's love, - God's love: flow from the Father through me.
Heaven's love, - God's love: flow for the whole world to see.
Heaven's love, - God's love: flow that like Christ we may be.
Heaven's love, - God's love: heaven's love.

Heaven's grace, - God's grace: flow from the Father through me.
Heaven's grace, - God's grace: flow for the whole world to see.
Heaven's grace, - God's grace: flow that like Christ we may be.
Heaven's grace, - God's grace: heaven's grace.

Heaven's peace, - God's peace: flow from the Father through me.
Heaven's peace, - God's peace: flow for the whole world to see.
Heaven's peace, - God's peace: flow that like Christ we may be.
Heaven's peace, - God's peace: heaven's peace.

1John 3:1,18

WOULD YOU QUEUE?

There are many queues I remember as a child of the forties. Some foods were in short supply or impossible to obtain and rationing was in force. The word would go round that there had been a delivery in town of tinned tomatoes or cans of jam from South Africa or Australia, or even oranges, a fruit I had never previously seen. Everyone would rush to the shop in question and a long queue would form. I also vividly recall when the whole school processed to the local clinic for each pupil to be inoculated against diseases prevalent at the time. This took place in a former mansion. We stood with knees knocking as the queue looped firstly around the large hall, then stretched up a huge winding staircase, along a gallery, eventually finishing in one of the rooms where a nurse rolled up our sleeves. The sight of a large needle filled us with fear. When life was returning to normality after the war years, I remember we also queued in the booking hall of the local railway station to buy our tickets for a trip to the seaside. There were queues for the cinema and queues are still the norm at Post Offices on pension day. When the head of the queue is eventually reached, whether the reward for waiting is an ice cream or the surgeon's scalpel, the result is almost certainly for our enjoyment, benefit or reward.

Job is perhaps the prime example of waiting with patience whilst suffering the greatest anguish imaginable but he was unsure of what he could expect at the end. His reward was the restoration of his fortune to the extent of a doubling of his previous possessions. James urges us to wait patiently for the Lord and stand firm to the end like Job. Would you?

Job 6:11; 42:10 James 5:7-11

ANSWERED PRAYER

We cannot count the days our hearts
Laid low in deep despair.
We only know You raised us up
In answer to our prayer;
Our feet fixed firmly to the rock:
Turned darkness into light:
A new song put upon our lips, -
A psalm for Your delight.

You did not ask for sacrifice
As deemed in days of old,
But that we bring our human hearts
Your glory to behold.
Your wonders and Your purposes,
Countless, beyond compare,
Created for the common good,
You shaped, for all to share.

Your goodness, hidden in our hearts,
We now affirm aloud,
But turn from those who spurn Your love, -
The arrogant and proud.
Yet may they hear Your words through us
And feel Your tender care?
Your constant love surrounds us, Lord.
Your goodness may they share.

So all who truly seek may find
Your saving, stretched-forth arm
Which lifts us, holds us, cares for us
And shelters us from harm.
"All glory to the Lord!" This song
To You we dedicate.
Your Kingdom come. Your reign of peace
We patiently await.

Psalm 40

THE SOUND OF SILENCE

The door of heaven stands open wide. Day following day and night following night, comes the unceasing sound of songs of praise to God, the Sovereign Lord. But the Lamb breaks the seventh seal and there is a silence in heaven for about half an hour. After this, a vast throng sing praises to the Lord God.

How curious! Silence for about half an hour. Why the need?

Is this silence for the prayers of the saints who have gone before or, indeed, for our own prayers? Or could it be to enable us to renew our energies for even greater praise? Is it a time set aside for reflection, to look back on all our wrongdoing, or on God's goodness in providing for our redemption? Is the time given for us to look forwards, to the reign of God commencing? Or is it akin to 'passport control' or whilst we are being fitted with new bodies and voices? Is it a time for eating heavenly, spiritual food in order to grow perfected in grace? Or is it a time when God Himself withdraws to pray for us, like when Jesus withdrew after feeding the five thousand?

Could this sound of silence be the Lord God Himself re-robing as King of Kings in the Robes of Victory?

Revelation 4:1-8; 8:1; 19:1,11-13

EARTH'S NEW SONG

Organ sound and choir sing
Songs of joy, to Christ, - the King!
Thankful voices fill the air.
Sing with gladness everywhere.

Cymbals crash, and trumpets blaze; -
Notes of adoration raise.
Melodies ring to the sky; -
Hearts and voices lift on high.

Advertise God's power of love,
How His Son came from above
To reveal the Father's care
For His children, everywhere.

Broadcast wide, Christ Jesu's name,
How to save this world He came.
Happy chords may then resound
As our God, through Christ, is found.

Loving kindness fill your heart:
Joyful words your lips impart:
Unashamed the Saviour praise:
Earth's new song for Jesus raise.

Hymns and psalms to Him belong:
Earth resound anew in song:
Organ, cymbals, trumpets, lyre,
With the one, eternal choir.

Psalm 149:1-3; 150:3-6

101

ALPHA & OMEGA

There's a beginning and end to all things but often we are never quite sure when a start is made or the end is reached. Abram, for example, probably never expected it would be the start of things when he heard the voice of the Lord at seventy years of age, but nevertheless obeyed and set out from Harran on a long and arduous journey to Canaan. Likewise, Moses would have been eighty when in response to God's call he led the children of Israel out of Egypt and it was another forty years before his eyes beheld the distant Promised Land which he himself could not enter. There are numerous other examples in the Bible of unexpected beginnings or endings.

It is unsurprising, therefore, to realise that this little booklet had its beginnings as long ago as 1970 when at the age of thirty the author wrote a poem as a result of having to stand and stare across at a cathedral building whilst sheltering from a heavy downpour and subsequently entering this poem in his own church magazine. Over the intervening years as the Spirit stirred within him thoughts provoked further poems until possibly thirty-five years later a conscious decision was made to write one last poem and this was to be as difficult a biblical task as possible. i.e. to paraphrase Psalm 23 in a completely new light. This appears as 'The Tables of Our Lord.'

But this did not prove to be the end of composition as towards Christmas 2008 as the author lay in bed with shingles, the words opposite came to mind in a matter of minutes and were hurriedly scribbled down whilst still in the memory. Is this the Omega! Only time will tell if this is God's will.

Genesis 12.1-4 Deuteronomy 34.7 Acts 7.3, 23, 30-36
Revelation 1.8; 21.6; 22.13

SHINGLE JINGLE

Which is the way to Bethlehem?
Just follow the bright guiding star.
Will I find there, a new-born king?
Yes. Find a stable door ajar.
How will I know that he's a king?
Ask to hear what the shepherds saw.
And will his crown be by his side?
See the wreath that's nailed to the door.

Which is the way from Bethlehem?
Just follow the steep thorny track.
But that path leads to Calvary?
Join him with the load on his back.
Where is this king then, on his throne?
Ask to hear what the women saw.
Gaze far above. You'll see his crown
And read 'Welcome' on heaven's door.

Matthew 2:1-10; 7:7,8,14; 16:24,28; Mark 8:34;
Luke 1:32-33: 2:8-18; 9:23,27; 11:9-10;
John 19:1-3; 21-27; 20:1,11-17 Revelation 3:20; 5:12-13

Whitby Abbey North Yorkshire

APPENDIX

ON A DONKEY'S BACK

I dreamt I was near Bethlehem.
The night was dark and cold.
I saw some shepherds huddled in
The entrance to their fold.

I mingled with the shepherds as
They gazed upon a star
Which shone above a stable there
And found its door ajar.

I had ridden on a donkey
Far up the mountain track.
I sat behind a darkened cross
He carried on his back.

I stood beside the donkey that
Had carried Mary there,
And glimpsed a cross upon its back,
But she was unaware.

The lambs were quietly sleeping with
The sheep, safe and secure.
No predator could penetrate;
The shepherds formed the door.

I wondered if the donkey knew
He bore this cross of pain,
And he would carry on his back
The Lamb that would be slain.

But suddenly the silence broke
As angels filled the sky.
The shepherds heard in wonderment
A message from on high.

But, 'Donkey, hold your head up high,
For proudly, you can say
The Babe you bore with Mary then
Will save the world one day.'

'Leave now, and go to Bethlehem'
Their joyful chorus rang;
'Go greet the new-born King of Peace'
The choirs of heaven sang.

I knelt there with the shepherds bowed
In awe before the King;
The King of Peace, whose endless reign
A peace unknown would bring.

THE CRUCIFIXION

Lord, let us trace those steps so drear
Winding their way up Calvary's hill;
Heavy the cross you had to bear:
Help us your load to carry still.

'Away with Him!' the cry rang out.
'Lead Him away!' and 'Crucify!'
Lord, do we 'Crucify!' still shout?
'Away with Him!' do we dare cry?
          ('The Son of God? Send Him to die?')

Nailed to the cross, in awful pain,
Jesus, despised, our sins did bear.
Mocked, jeered, afflicted, yet no stain
Was on the Lamb as He hung there.

Jesus, in shame and sorrow deep,
Died, yet to pardon those who call.
There on the cross could Christ still weep
'Father, forgive; forgive them all.'

Lonely Redeemer, hanging there
Forsaken by your closest friends:
Lord, in that anguish let us share:
Know that your love, all loves transcends.

Your crown of thorns, Lord, let us feel,
One spike, one touch of bitter pain.
Through death the perfect life reveal.
Jesus, our Lord, died not in vain!

From depth of gloom, the final hour
Broke forth into eternal day.
Yours is the kingdom, Yours the power,
The joy, the truth, the light, the way!

THE FIRST APOSTLES

Thanks to God for Simon Peter,
    Mighty rock on which to build!
Given the keys of heaven to Peter,
    Jesu's promise he fulfilled.
Peter, sure, so firm and steadfast
Heads the march of saints who at last
    Conquer death as first God willed.

Thanks to God for Luke and Matthew
    Whose great gospels we hold dear,
Telling of the life of Jesus,
    Words that make His purpose clear.
Faithful men whose records cheer us,
Share with us the truths of Jesus.
    Worthy men with hearts sincere.

Thanks to our Father God for John.
    Keen preceptor of the Light:
Jesus, unknown, unaccepted,
    Whose love lights the darkest night.
John stood witness to a brightness,
Truth, arrayed in dazzling whiteness
    Off'ring man a new birthright.

Thanks to God for Martyr Stephen
    With the Holy Spirit filled.
Bold in speech with strong conviction,
    Christ's first witness to be killed.
Stephen stood his ground proclaiming
Jesus King, despite the stoning
    And in death, forgiveness willed.

Thanks to God for Apostle Paul,
    Traveller far, the church to teach.
Paul's great words of Christ's salvation
    Drew the crowds to hear him preach.
Paul, whose written words inspiring,
For his Lord lived, never tiring.
    Urged the church's outward reach.

THE FAMILY OF GOD

Brothers and sisters, parents and child,
Heirs of salvation to God reconciled!
Children, from God no longer to roam,
Longing to reach our heavenly home.

       God is the Father, God is the Son.
       God is the Spirit, the Three in One.
       God is the Giver of Life so free.
       God is the Lover of you and me.

Listen, my children. God's word is true.
Christ has prepared such a welcome for you.
Someone to shoulder troubles and care.
God given blessings we can all share.

       God is .....

Brothers and sisters, united be,
Enter God's house as one family,
Living for ever as Jesus taught,
United in purpose, united in thought.

       God is .....

God, the Provider of all of our needs;
Jesus, our Saviour, with heavenly food feeds;
Spirit of Comfort, Spirit to guide,
He will walk always right by our side.

       God is .....

God our Creator, his image to show;
Christ our Redeemer, truly we know.
God through his Son reclaiming his own;
Spirit the Truth, the Word to make known.

THE POET'S ANGUISH

Battered bodies; bloodstained field;
Crumbled houses; charred remains:
Fever, havoc, stench from drains; (panic, havoc reigns;)
Anguish, wailing; spirits yield.

Toppled timbers; rank rubble;
Debris, dust, dense choking smoke:
Ruined hopes; crestfallen folk;
Shattered lives; endless trouble.

Frightened folk; frenzied faces;
Screaming mothers; dogs run wild:
Brutal killings, old man, child;
Such sourness war embraces.

Nameless dead; communal graves;
Strong men faint whilst women weep:
Mass destruction; lives are cheap.
Man destroys but Jesus saves!

The Tenterden Methodist Church WW1 Memorial Pipe Organ

GOD THE COMFORTER

When I'm all alone
    And I'm living with pains and sorrows,
Bemoaning wretched todays
    And even worse tomorrows,
Whose voice whispers in my ear,
Makes my heart leap, gives me cheer,
Proving I need have no fear?
    Why, God's alone!

When I'm down and out
    And my heart has that sinking feeling,
Everything seems distasteful
    And life has lost all meaning,
Whose love reaches out to me
Making me feel glad and free,
So happy, it's plain to see?
    Why, God's alone!

When I get things wrong
    And my heart is filled with guilt and shame,
Nothing will ever go right
    And I am always to blame,
Whose firm hand slips into mine,
Disperses clouds for sunshine,
Makes me brave and feel so fine?
    Why, God's alone!

SELFISHNESS

If all the saints of ages past
Could hear the way I pray!
So many times I place God last:
I pray a selfish way.
His wrath should be like some great storm;
Waves in a raging sea.
But God is Love. His love so warm
Like sunshine glows on me.

If all the saints who went before
Could see how now we build;
Penthouses on the seventeenth floor
And homes with 'must have' filled!
With all we have, we still want more.
Those saints would grieve to scan
Our pleasures, whilst we still ignore
Our starving brother, man.

If all our forefathers could speed
As fast as we go now;
Such speed to keep us in the lead
In eagerness for power!
If they could see a rocket bound
For some far distant star,
Would they not say 'God's peace is found
So near. Why go so far?'.

PETITIONARY PRAYER

What joy to step in church and kneel
To offer silent prayer
To God, whose nearness there I feel.
I know that He is there.
My God will hear the words I say,
He'll soothe my troubled mind,
And when I reach the close of day
His promised rest I'll find.

Please listen, Lord, while I confess
The many times I cheat, (sin)
And lift me up from my distress
And set me on my feet. (cleanse my heart within.)
Make me aware that your deep love
Is even meant for me
And when I reach your courts (my home) above
Your welcome smile I'll see.

My God, I ask that I may be
Your servant from this night.
Wipe my slate clean, my heart set free;
In future so choose right.
May I, Lord, ever walk your way
And others strive to win,
And when I come home hear you say
'True servant, enter in.'

The shadow of the cross I see
And tears I can't suppress.
My Saviour's love has changed for me
Despair to happiness.
In this quiet hour of prayer, Lord, send
The Comforter to me.
And when I reach my journey's end,
My God I know I'll see.

THE KING OF CREATION HERALD'S HIS QUEEN

Composer, Conductor of the Work Supreme;
The King of Creation heralds now His Queen!
The sun streams a brilliant overture of light;
Day patterns harmonise length'ning shades of night.
Soft mellow sunshine seeks out the rainbow's arch;
Thunder and lightning proclaim Christ's victory march.
Mountains and ocean depths sound symphonic chords;
Earth completes the chorus for the Lord of Lords.
Composer, Conductor of the Work Supreme;
The King of Creation heralds now His Queen!

INDEX of BIBLICAL TEXTS

INDEX of BIBLICAL TEXTS

INDEX of BIBLICAL TEXTS

INDEX of BIBLICAL TEXTS

INDEX of BIBLICAL TEXTS

INDEX of BIBLICAL TEXTS

INDEX of BIBLICAL TEXTS

INDEX of BIBLICAL TEXTS

INDEX of BIBLICAL TEXTS

Lightning Source UK Ltd.
Milton Keynes UK
UKHW021659050122
396606UK00006B/73